D0861969

TALESPINS
A Story of Early Aviation Days

Edith Dodd Culver

Sunstone Press
Santa Fe, New Mexico

Dedicated
to
The Early Birds of Aviation
and to
The Air Mail Pioneers

Acknowledgement

I wish to acknowledge the generous assistance which Reuben H. Fleet
has given me by allowing me to quote from his booklet "Fifty Years
of Air Mail," and for the use of some of his pictures.

E.D.C.

First Edition

Printed in the United States of America

Library of Congress Cataloging in Publication Data:

Culver, Edith Dodd.
    Talespins: A story of early aviation days.

    Includes index.
    1. Aeronautics--United States--History. I. Title.
TL521.C77   1985   629.13'0973   85-17359
ISBN: 0-86534-073-0

Published in 1986 by SUNSTONE PRESS
        Post Office Box 2321
        Santa Fe, NM 87504-2321 / USA

C O N T E N T S

Preview
5

CHAPTER 1
The Early Years
16

CHAPTER 2
Princeton
28

CHAPTER 3
Dayton
35

CHAPTER 4
Houston
39

CHAPTER 5
First Aerial Mail
42

CHAPTER 6
Armistice
70

CHAPTER 7
In The Beginning
74

CHAPTER 8
The Curtiss School
85

CHAPTER 9
Captain Baldwin
94

CHAPTER 10
Other Pioneers
99

CHAPTER 11
Talespins
104

CHAPTER 12
The Early Birds
110

CHAPTER 13
The Golden Anniversary
119

Index
126

Preview

The time has come to say something about the women in aviation who flew the first primitive airplanes; and also about the ones who were silent partners of the men who pioneered the air and space age from Jennies to Jets to Rockets, and of the part they played in the development of these marvels of the twentieth century.

Imagine, if you can, a time when women were not welcome at flying fields — not even as spectators. Something might go wrong, there might be an accident and there often were, a crackup or even a fatality — and the "delicate" female must be spared this shock. Accidents were hard enough on stouthearted men, but after all they were the ones doing the experimenting with an entirely new thing called a flying machine. These pioneers were just learning how to keep a frail craft made of wood, wire and fabric up in the air and what horsepower engine to use to accomplish it. It did not occur to anyone that this was anything but man's work and several hundred courageous and adventurous young men took up the challenge after the Wright brothers accomplished powered flight on December 17, 1903 at Kitty Hawk, North Carolina.

In the exciting thirteen years that followed this world-shaking event, everyone wanted to share in the action. Those closest to it kept records, logs, blueprints, newspaper and magazine articles about their exploits, autograph books in which famous flyers had signed their names and they collected and saved all sorts of memorabilia — even old airplanes.

In the years following, a group of old timers decided something should be done to preserve these priceless historical treasures for posterity, as well as to have a reason to get together for annual meetings where they could indulge in their favorite pasttime — rocking chair flying. So in 1928 a group of those pioneers organized an exclusive club to be known as The Early Birds of Aviation. The requirement for membership was proof that the candidate had flown solo before December 17, 1916. Pilot's licenses were issued early on and if one did not possess such a credential, he was required to have a bona fide witness vouch for him.

Notice went out and the membership role began to grow. At the top of the list were two honorary names — Orville and Wilbur Wright. Unfortunately Wilbur Wright had died of typhoid fever on May 30, 1912, at the age of 45, cutting short a remarkable career in partnership with his brother Orville with whom he had made a dynamic discovery that led mankind into the air age. Orville lived on for many years continuing their work. And he sometimes joined the Early Birds at meetings. I recall the one held at Ford's Greenfield Village at Dearborn, Michigan which at one time had housed some of the Early Bird collection, and where the Wright bicycle shop now stands. Ordinarily Orville Wright was a quiet man who kept aloof from the social scene at Hawthorn Hill, his home at Dayton, where he spent his later years. He passed away in January, 1945 in his 76th year. They are gone now but certainly not forgotten for the amazing accomplishments of those two industrious Dayton lads were to alter the course of civilization and change the world.

As soon as names began to be added to the Early Bird roster, officers were elected and regular sessions were held in different cities across the country. Members brought their trophies to the meetings and often brought their wives and families too. I remember poring over the fascinating scrapbooks and pictures in the Hospitality Room where we would congregate and talk over old times. It was plain that there should be a permanent repository for those priceless mementos, and steps were taken to find a suitable place. Several offers were made and tried out. But after being moved from place to place, a permanent home for the collection was finally found in the best of all places — the Smithsonian Institution. This was accomplished mainly through the invaluable influence of one of its own Early Bird members, Paul E. Garber. He had been on the staff there for years, and was the prime motive power in preserving aviation history from the beginning. He is the Early Bird archivist as well as Museum Curator Emeritus — and the Paul E. Garber facility was named for him. That is a well-deserved honor for that distinguished and well-loved Early Bird and air mail man. The Paul E. Garber Preservation, Restoration and Storage Facility is located at nearby Suitland, Maryland where it houses the National Air and Space Museum's reserve collection of historically significant air and space craft. On display are some 90 aircraft as well as numerous spacecraft engines, propellers and other flight-related objects which have been preserved mainly due to Paul's vigilance. His wife, Irene, better known as "Buttons" could be called Mrs. Early Bird, so close has she been to all of this. She came by it naturally through her mother known as Mother Tusch because of her interest in aviation and her friendship with so many aviators in the early days.

All the Early Bird material, bibliographies, and portfolios are now stored in fireproof containers in a special room under constant guard. There is a gallery called "Early Flight" which displays material from prior to World War I and it includes Early Bird mementos. But the most popular things on display are in the Great Hall of the Air and Space Museum, where such famous airplanes as the "Kitty Hawk," Wright's original plane, Lindbergh's "Spirit of St. Louis," Wiley Post's "Winnie May" and many others hang suspended as though in flight.

Another display in the gallery is a large bronze Early Bird plaque where more than five hundred names are preserved for all time. Women's names are there, too, for by that time the old taboo and prejudice against women flyers had disappeared.

A handsome individual bronze plaque, a small replica of the large one, is awarded to each Early Bird on the fiftieth anniversary of his or her solo flight, and presented with an appropriate ceremony at the Early Bird reunion. The plaque shows the winged Early Bird insignia, the aviator's name and the date of his solo flight and signed with the Early Bird's of Aviation legal signature.

I am proud to know that the name of my late husband, H. Paul Culver is engraved on those memorial plaques along with the names of many of our friends who, like Paul, were also airmail pilots. These early aviators were dauntless, resourceful and scientifically inclined when dealing with such an undeveloped and inexact science. It was a trial and error period, and failure could mean both a human and financial tragedy. The memorial plaque serves to remind us what we owe our aviation pioneers for it represents the slow, difficult years when aviation was growing up. It might not have survived but for those pioneers who persisted until the idea caught on and grew into the incredible giant it is today.

In the beginning the Early Birds of Aviation was to be "last man organization" but in 1976 that was changed to give it permanent status. It seemed fitting to grant the title of Associate Member to their families and to those who are interested in perserving pioneer aviation. Associate members now enjoy this unique honor and perhaps in this way the Early Bird tradition will survive long after the originals are gone. The Associates now hold offices and participate in the annual meetings along with the original Early Birds who still attend although in ever dwindling numbers. To date, there are only 21 originals left, and only 3 attended the 1984 reunion. By contrast pilots licenses number into the thousands — even to over a million! But it was these very men who in their youth were the ones who ventured into the bold new world of aviation which drew its ranks from every strata of society.

It called for the skill of the inventor, the engineer, the mechanic, the innovator, and for courageous young men to do the actual testing and flying. It was the latter who drew the most attention and publicity in the early days for there was an aura about the pioneer aviator much like that of the early movie actor of the silent screen. He was idolized as a romantic hero and some of them apparently enjoyed and lived up to the role. The press did its part as it does today, and a real journalistic scoop was to feature a picture of a handsome aviator clad in leather flying suit, with helmet and goggles in hand, posed nonchalantly beside a Curtiss Biplane or Flying boat. The accompanying story about his aerial and terrestrial exploits touched the heart of many a local maiden, and mash notes, invitations, a rabbit's foot to hang on the cowl for luck, and religious medals for divine protection poured in, and even fan clubs were organized. But frankly, most of the flyers could care less. They were too busy. It was my happy lot to know many of these lads and to live among them at the various fields where we were stationed.

Of course, there were women in the lives of these young men who played their part if only in the background or behind the scenes. These were the wives and sweethearts and the hangers-on and camp followers, but it was the aviatrix that claimed the spotlight. She was the one who had the audacity to come to an all-male airfield and break down a barrier by taking flying lessons on an equal footing with men. And how she has proved herself! It has seemed to take the perspective of time to place her in her proper niche in aviation history.

But the life of the Early Bird wife was much less exciting. She was definitely not a part of the action. Since she was excluded from the flying field at first, her role was to simply keep the home fires burning — so to speak — to stay at home and like any housewife of that generation, to cook and sew, mind the children and perform her patriotic duty by knitting sweaters for the soldiers fighting overseas, and pray for the fledglings over at the flying field. Her quarters were close enough to hear the sound of a motor overhead and when it sputtered or quit she could only hope the plane would land safely. It was a lonely vigil except for the time she spent with the other wives with whom she could discuss mutual worries and frustrations, and exchange the scuttlebutt their husbands brought home from the field. This was pleasant camaraderie for young women and it laid the foundation for several lifelong friendships with such fine Early Bird wives as Charlotte Vernon, wife of Victor Vernon who was chief flying instructor at the school at that time, and Loa Lees, wife of Walter E. Lees, chief instructor on the Curtiss flying boat. Loa and I had been childhood chums and fate brought us together again to resume a close friendship that continued from the time when our husbands became staff members at the Atlantic Coast Experimental Station and Curtiss Flying School at Newport News, Virginia in 1916. It was the largest and most active aviation facility in the United States at the time.

As time went on wives could put in an appearance at the school especially on Sundays when the public was allowed to visit and watch the flying. That brought them closer to the actual picture. And to realize their obligation: always keep their cool no matter what happened, and to keep their morale high because a wife's attitude could make or break her husband's career. They accepted that responsibility and lived up to it. Those who did not soon disappeared from the scene. Flying was dangerous business and it took a certain kind of woman to be the wife of an Early Bird or an airmail pilot. It wasn't all just romance.

At first flying was only done with the field in plain view, but soon flyers began to venture out of range of the field and at greater altitudes — all without compass or parachute — and to land miles from home base in clearings of any kind. That was part of the advanced training course and it brought new worries to their wives. By this time cross-country airmail routes were established by night and day and it brought the acid test to the wives of our airmail pilots. It was not easy to see her man take off to blaze uncertain trails across the sky. It took real courage and stamina to sit out many anxious hours, much like watching our men go off to war.

Incredibly we have never properly honored our airmail pilots nor the women in their lives who bravely backed them up. Those pilots risked their lives and careers to build the world's first and best airmail service, which led the way in creating a dependable, scheduled routine that became the basis for our great commercial aviation industry. Let's not forget that.

It was just such an attitude on the part of women that led one of them, Katharine Wright, the school teacher sister of the Wright brothers, to offer her meager earnings to help them finance their first experiments. They still say in Dayton, Ohio, their home town, that "without Kitty Wright there wouldn't have been any Kitty Hawk." It is heart warming to know that she lived to see her brothers' success and fame at home and abroad and to share in it. I'm sure there are many unsung heroines in the annals of aviation so I deeply regret any omissions or oversight.

However, I knew a few of the earliest women flyers well. They either taught themselves to fly or had the gumption to enroll at the all-male school and earn a pilot's license. After they completed the course they were off to fly at County Fairs, to do barnstorming or exhibition flying to advertise products of the few aircraft manufacturers, and even to compete in cross-country air races, and to fly the mail for Uncle Sam. They were paid well for these services, too. There must have been times when conventional women envied the courage and freedom of their winged sisters and wished to break out of the mold into which they were poured because of their sex. Aviation was a new and exciting field for women and the daring ones grasped it even if it was not considered ladylike or proper. But neither was anything else that did not conform to tradition. It was acceptable to marry and raise a family, teach school, be a secretary or clerk in a store or just do nothing, but it was not quite respectable to go into such professions as law, medicine or nursing, or sports except perhaps tennis, golf or croquet. It was nothing short of scandalous to go on the stage, and woe unto the woman who divorced her husband — she was a social outcast. Women were not even allowed to vote at that time nor did anyone dream of a woman's liberation movement although Sylvia Pankhurst had come over from London and was being heard by a select group of young ladies at Milwaukee Downer College for Women where I was a student. I heard her say that the new woman was emerging over the horizon, if only faintly and that the sheltered life syndrome was doomed.

Little did I dream that I was to see this prophecy come to pass, nor that after I had seen my first airplane in the sky that a spark was kindled which was to glow into a lifelong fascination with aviation.

It began at my hometown County Fair in 1911, where from my place in the grandstand I watched spellbound, though with some trepidation, while a handsome young Curtiss exhibition flyer flew figure eights above the race track. Only the bravest of men would attempt such a hazardous feat. The fair maidens of our town were all agog, for now they had a new hero to idolize — Beckwith Havens, and Douglas Fairbank's name was relegated to second place by our local fan club.

It was not until 1913 that I saw a sensational front page picture in the Milwaukee Sentinel that I could hardly believe. A woman dared do the same thing. There she was — Blanche Stuart Scott — and she even dressed like an aviator. That seemed pretty bold, especially the knee length knickerbockers which showed her legs below the knee. At that time legs were completely covered down to the ankle — but after all what would the wind do to long skirts in the open cockpit of a Curtiss Pusher? But her picture accompanied a tragic story — she had wrecked her plane at the Madison Wisconsin Fairgrounds and had been rushed to a hospital. Her flight was the main attraction and people had come from miles around. She had even flown a few turns over the city where people rushed into the streets to see this strange sight in the sky. Having returned to the fairground and taking a turn over the race track she lost control and came down in a tangled heap of wood, wire and fabric. But after many weeks of convalescence she was back in the harness again. The fine living she made flying was too good to give up. Later, I met Blanche at an Early Bird reunion and I asked her about that experience. She remembered it well and added that she believed that every bone in her body had been broken in that crackup.

That was my first encounter with women who flew and it was grim, but later on I was to meet another one and be pleasantly surprised. One fall day in 1916, folks at the Curtiss school were startled to see a strange airplane appear out of the blue, glide down and land on a nearby farmer's field and taxi over to the hanger and ask to have the mechanics check over her plane. She had flown in from New York unannounced in those days before radio to have her engine checked in preparation for entering a cross-country race from New York to Chicago. It was one of the first such air races and the high stakes for the winner were attractive. It was their first lady customer so naturally they were glad to oblige but her presence created quite a stir. Her name was Ruth Law. Following this period she had a long and colorful career in aviation and was one of the first Early Birds. No doubt her example gave impetus to the woman's movement in the early days. She lived to see most female barriers broken down and fade away.

Then there was Katherine Stinson, youngest of the famous Stinson flying family whose enterprising mother had sparked their careers by starting a flying school of her own in Texas from which her children graduated. I first met Katherine in October, 1916. She was giving exhibitions of night flying at the State Fairgrounds in Richmond, Virginia. Everyone at the Curtiss School was curious to see this unusual performance. We were too, so my husband and I boarded an old stern-wheeler steamboat and took the all day trip up the James River to see the show. One stop en route was at the old church at Jamestown. That was about all that was there and a kindly caretaker showed us about the quiet and deserted grounds. Reaching Richmond at dusk we hurried out to the fairgrounds and when it got dark enough, Katherine made her spectacular flight, circling the fairgrounds several times. The magnesium flares (like Fourth of July Roman candles) attached to the wing tips glowed eerily against the black sky as the crowd applauded and the band played to heighten the effect. She glided gently back to earth to a spot lighted and marked by bonfires. What a thrill! We were pleasantly surprised with Katherine for instead of the tomboy we had expected, she was dainty and as friendly as the "girl next door." Her publicity agents called her the Flying School Girl or the more glamorous title "America's Sweetheart of the Air." She seemed to fit both titles perfectly. She wore long curls like Mary Pickford (who was then America's sweetheart of the silent screen) but Katherine tucked her curls into the boy's cap that she wore with the visor reversed. She was dressed like a boy in shirt and pants — not the tight jeans that modern women wear, but voluminous knickerbockers like gym bloomers. Long black cotton stockings and tennis shoes completed her outfit.

Our pleasant encounter with Katherine led to a friendship that we resumed at Early Bird meetings and later when she gave up flying altogether for a domestic role, becoming Mrs. Michael Otero of Santa Fe, New Mexico. She had a remarkable flying career that took her all over the United States and the Orient where she was feted and showered with trophies and gifts. She even flew the United States mail for a period. She had done it all — a true pioneer.

As the years rolled along it no longer seemed strange for women to fly. A great levelling was taking place in all walks of life. Women were proving themselves in every field of endeavor, but it still takes a certain type to take to the air. They deserve special attention and thousands of them have earned their wings. They have their own associations such as the Ninety-Nines and the Powder Puff Derbies, they have gone into the military, into government and have gone international. Perhaps that is the reason that no one was too surprised when one of their sisters was selected to be part of an all male crew aboard a spaceship rocket. No doubt one of them will walk on the moon some day. "You've come a long way, baby" is a popular phrase that certainly applies to modern woman. More power to her!

At a recent Early Bird gathering held in cooperation with the OX-5 Aviation Pioneers organization, some of the most interesting speeches were given by women pilots telling of their experiences — something unheard of in the early days but nowadays entirely natural. I am sure that the few other Early Bird widows who were present, like I, only regretted that their husbands were not there to observe with us the fact that the air age has advanced into space and that it had gone coed. But the Early Birds also gave a good accounting of themselves. They always did. Old aviators never bow out nor do they just fade away but continue to delight audiences with tales of the old days which not only entertain but are of great historical value. There is a special spirit in such men that glows to the end.

Looking back, it is no wonder that my Victorian parents could not believe their ears when in 1916 I announced my intentions to marry an aviator (in those days you did not marry without your parent's consent). When they had recovered from the shock and after trying to talk me out of it they became reconciled and gave their consent provided I would promise to stay on the ground myself. Thus began a most thrilling and exciting few years that I shall always cherish. I kept that promise for some years and I did stay on the ground — looking up.

Time has gone swiftly by since the twentieth century was ushered in by many miraculous and revolutionary ideas. Greater development and more radical changes were to come about than in all the history of mankind preceeding it. Great inventions were to come upon the scene and I wish to start with the Wright brothers, and *Aviation* because the discovery of controlled powered flight lifted mankind out of its earth bound status and set research into new paths, away from a material sense of limitation into greater freedom of thought and accomplishment. The great powers of the universe have been tamed and made practical beyond our wildest dreams. Rockets are king now.

We used to think that the heavenly bodies had a private and un-disturbed realm of their own until our space rockets began to probe into their domain, but I am sure our invasion has not disturbed their per-manence nor luster any more than Halley's comet will in its 75 year cir-cuits. In 1985 it shed its radiance on a very different world than in 1910. Well do I remember being awed and a bit frightened by its appearance then. It has been my privilege to have lived during that span of years and to marvel at the changes. One cannot help but wonder what kind of world Halley's comet will look down upon its next time around.

The story of pioneer aviation in America has been told by historian, journalist and personal authors and now I wish to tell mine which has been gleaned from my diary and because I had the rare privilege of being a pioneer aviator wife. The time has come to remind ourselves that there was thrill and romance in aviation long before Lindbergh and our other national aviation heros were heard of.

I have had a wonderful time reliving all of the vignettes that follow, and if some of the stories seem to overlap or I repeat at times, it is only to emphasize a point that seemed important to me. Because the air mail story seemed the most important historically, I begin with it.

1
The Early Years

Army orders were no surprise to the wife of a pioneer Army aviator. She just packed and moved on to the next Post, grateful her husband hadn't been ordered overseas. Wives could not go along in 1918 during World War I. But War Department orders #102 dated May 1, 1918 were different because they meant my husband First Lieutenant H. Paul Culver was to be temporarily relieved of his duty at Ellington Field, Houston, Texas and loaned to the Post Office Department to fly the First Aerial Mail.

No wonder I was pleased because it postponed the overseas duty for which Paul was slated. But he was not happy over the assignment. He did not dream it would give him a niche in history, nor would he have cared. He had no idea why he had been selected. Didn't his credentials qualify him for more important duty than a routine mail-carrying job? He was an Early Bird, an aviation pioneer who had soloed before December 17, 1916; he had a diploma from the Curtiss Flying School, Newport News, Virginia, which showed he had graduated from there on September 1, 1916, after soloing on the Curtiss F-boat; he had soloed on the Curtiss "Jenny" on October 15, 1916 and had qualified for Aero Club of America pilots license #673, and for experts license #74. He had been a test pilot, an aviation engineering officer, a flying instructor at several Army fields, and he had been one of the first five aviators to receive training in the Signal Corps Officers Reserve Corps program when that course was initiated at Newport News in 1916. Wasn't his experience working with Glenn Curtiss and Captain Thomas Baldwin at the Atlantic Coast Aeronautical Experimental Station worth something more important than flying the mail, he reasoned? Was he to scrap all that know-how now for such uninteresting duty, especially when his one wish had been to go overseas and do his part toward winning the war?

This unexpected and unusual order came to Paul during an intensive period of teaching an advanced class of war pilots on the acrobatic stage at Ellington. He was busy with this program along with his duties as

Commanding officer of the 189th Aero Squadron. And he had been training aviators for combat flying on the Western Front in Europe even before the summer of 1917, when the United States joined with its European allies in a war that was supposed to make the world safe for democracy.

Acrobatic flying taught student aviators the skills they would need in aerial combat such as looping the loop, side slipping, banking and doing the Immelman turn, and how to get out of the dreaded tailspin. They would need to know all these maneuvers in order to dodge enemy airplanes and bullets. When the student was ready to be turned loose for his solo, Paul and the other instructors had to supervise, observe and correct him before giving him his approval. This kept them busy from morning until night, and even during the night after several French aviators arrived at Ellington to teach night flying.

The French government sent us some its best pilots who were to give our aviators pointers on aerial combat tactics, and on night flying from their own experiences. The arrival of a group called the Blue Devils attracted much attention, especially their snappy blue uniforms topped with blue berets worn jauntily over one eye. Quite a contrast to the olive drab uniform and brown shoes of our army. We were equally impressed by the two dashing French ace Pilots, Aviateurs Lieutenant DeMandrot and Charles DeBony DeLa Vergne who arrived about the same time. Night flying instruction then began in earnest.

As the war accelerated, pilots were turned out at a rapid rate and there was no let up in the training schedule, day or night. Accustomed as we were at Ellington Field to hear the steady drone of motors overhead, yet the eerie sound of this new phase of aviation, night flying, with the sound of invisible airplanes in the darkness, was something we found hard to get used to. Sometimes their landing wheels seemed almost to graze our roof top when they skimmed low on their approach to the landing strip as the pilot maneuvered to set his airplane down between the row of lights spread out along the field to guide him. More than once were we started out of a sound sleep when a pilot overhead gave it the gun in order to miss our quarters and to pull up to circle and again aim for the landing field. We lived too close to the flying field for comfort!

One night a training plane plowed into the roof of one of the nearby hangars making what was known in aviation parlance as a "permanent"landing. Miraculously the pilot was not injured. He climbed down the ladder hoisted up to rescue him, somewhat dazed and chagrined by his failure to gauge his landing correctly, and retired to try again another night.

Another near-tragedy occurred one night when a dancing party was in progress at the Officer's Club. Suddenly we heard a loud crash. The orchestra stopped playing abruptly and everyone rushed into the darkness, fearing the worst. We saw the tail protruding from a nearby ditch, dust settling around it. The airplane was a shambles and the aviators stunned but neither seriously hurt. Fortunately the pilot had presence of mind to cut the switch before they hit. Otherwise the plane would have burst into flame and it would have been a different story. Soon the tow truck arrived to drag the twisted wreckage over to the repair shop and we all went back into the Club House to resume waltzing to the current popular theme song "Beautful Lady" from the operetta "Pink Lady," and two-stepping to "K-K-K-Katy," and other familiar hit tunes of the day.

The pioneer aviator was not always that lucky and we wives knew it, and felt the tension in the atmosphere as the pace of flying activity quickened. If you think the wife of the pioneer aviator was scared, you are right, for she knew how fragile those early airplanes were and she knew about the hazards. But she also realized the thrill of this new adventure, the conquest of the air. She saw her husband take off in a flimsy contraption made of wood, wire and linen whose framework supported the engine and the wooden propeller which delivered the horsepower to pull the frail craft into the air. (One of those wooden propellers now hangs on our wall, a nostalgic reminder of those "dear dead days beyond recall.") The engine and prop located in the nose of the Curtiss Jennies often became the lethal weapon which took the life of the pilot in a landing accident, especially if he was in the front seat of the tandem seating arrangement of the early training airplanes. The padded cowl surrounding both open cockpits was supposed to absorb some of the shock in case of a crash, but it was only a token device which made one feel better just to see it there.

However, the motor in the early flying boat was exposed and suspended directly above the head of pilot and passenger, like the Sword of Damocles. Pilots sat side by side in a waterproofed fuselage made of plywood which was certainly more substantial than the land airplane, but in case of a crash in the water, it was usually a complete wash out. I had seen this happen more than once at the Curtiss Flying School, when an F-boat or amphibian crash landed.

Because of my personal experiences in those pioneer years I can appreciate the stresses and strains our modern astronauts' wives have had to endure. They have expressed courage, enthusiasm and faith in their husbands ability, proving they are in tune with the project and that they have steeled themselves against any eventuality. They evidently realize that "they also serve who only stand and wait." Well do they know that the right attitude on the wife's part is the spirit which the husband catches subconsciously. Like the astronaut's wife, the pioneer aviator's wife had to realize that her husband was doing the thing he wanted to do and was happy in it. That was all she needed to know.

Fortunately for the astronauts' wives, they were born and raised in the air and space age, and as Army and Navy wives they have been groomed for the role they must play. Their close association with both aviation and the space project, and with all the personnel, as well as with the other wives whose husbands are also being trained for space exploration knits them up with the project. To be sure the pioneer aviator's wife did not have to endure the terrific tension of the count-down, which the modern astronaut's wife must experience when she watches on TV, along with the rest of the world, as her husband is rocketed into outer space. But she does have the assurance that the entire operation has been worked out with mathematical precision in the space laboratories. That is much different from the guess-work and mere individual trial-and-error of pioneer aviation. Moreover, the astronaut's wife has lived right in the NASA Community, and has been briefed on its every phase so that she feels a part of the team.

The pioneer aviator's wife had no such assurance. She lived apart from the Flying School and was an unwelcome visitor there because of frequent crack ups. Moreover, she was often the only woman around. It has been fascinating for me to watch from the sidelines as the air age has grown from Jennies to Jets to Rockets. If we once used the old cliche "I'd as soon try to fly" we now see a large segment of the human race up in the air all the time. And if we who once thought the sky was the limit, we now see the current generation reaching for the moon and beyond. Sometimes this all seems strange to me who was born and raised in the horse and buggy era and can still remember when the first automobile came to our town, to say nothing of the excitement of seeing the first airplane in 1911. At that time, anything off the ground was outerspace.

Our quarters #58-A at Ellington Field in 1918 were directly across a narrow gravel road from the Field Hospital and our neighbors on officer's row were mostly the personnel and physicians on duty there. A medical atmosphere was not foreign to me because I had been brought up in my father's hospital in Ashland, Wisconsin and was no stranger to the sights, sounds and smells of sickness and accident. But this was different! Not only could I hear the shrill siren of the Field ambulance as it rushed a casualty to the emergency entrance but I could also see the limp figure in tan leather jacket, puttees and helmet, as it was hurriedly carried inside. "Could it be Paul?" It could, because all aviators dressed alike in those days and I couldn't tell one from the other on that stretcher from across the street, and I could not dash frantically over to the emergency ward every time this happened. We were at war, I must remember that! A lot of hysterical wives at a flying field would be as bad for morale as enemy sabotage. I had learned that lesson early from Captain Thomas Baldwin, who was the manager of the Curtiss Flying School where Paul learned to fly, and where I arrived as a bride in 1916. He discouraged my visits to the field at first, lest I should be nervous when Paul was in the air. But I soon persuaded him that my nerves were steady, and to prove it, he arranged a flight for me in Victor Vernon's flying boat to test my mettle. I passed with "flying colors" and was then allowed to visit the school whenever I chose.

The Early Years

Later on when I lived full-time on an Army Aviation Post along with many other wives, we were briefed on suitable behavior and esprit de corps, especially at the Red Cross meetings which were held regularly on the Post. We wives would gather there to roll bandages, make surgical dressings, knit and chat. I'm sure each woman there breathed a silent prayer, as she worked on those medical supplies, that her husband would never need the dressings she was making. But she was glad to do her part and to be of service in the war effort, and the hospital certainly needed all the dressings we could provide for just such emergencies as the accidents which I so often observed from my quarters.

One day I was to learn right away who the unconscious figure on the stretcher was. The Field ambulance sped up to the hospital entrance with two stretchers and at the same moment I heard our back door click shut. It seems that Paul had tried to slip in that way, unnoticed, before I should be aware of his presence, or see his mud and blood spattered uniform. I followed him into the bathroom, speechless with anxiety, when I saw him, although it flashed through my mind that because he had come home under his own power, he couldn't be badly hurt. That was some comfort and at least it wasn't Paul on one of those stretchers! As soon as he had washed up and changed his uniform and caught his breath, he told me what had happened: one of his best friends from his early flying days, flight instructor Earl Southee, had just crashed on the edge of the field where Paul was giving a group of students a lecture on acrobatic flying. Seeing Earl's plane crash head first into a nearby ditch, they had all rushed over and found him and his student unconscious and badly injured. The Field ambulance which with the fire truck was always near at hand, came alongside and Paul and his students helped the interns extricate the two casualties and place them on stretchers. Then Paul came in from the field on his motorcycle. It seems that Earl's student had frozen on the controls, and he had been unable to shake him loose. The student hung on like grim death and both of them rode the airplane into the ground head first, burying the motor deep into the earth. The student was hurt the least because he was in the back seat but Earl, in the front seat received the full force of the impact, and as a result spent many weary months in the hospital. Traction, plastic surgery and skin grafting were involved in his recovery. The doctors fixed him up so that he was as handsome as ever even minus one eyebrow. He told us how this happened: the surgeon took a small slice from the back of Earl's neck where the hair and skin was of similar texture and had grafted it on in the place of the missing eyebrow, but it didn't adhere, and Earl's story is that when he was given medical leave to visit his home in Binghamton, New York he went up to New York City for a little fun and gayety by way of change of pace. While there he attended the Ziefgeld Follies and he laughed so hard his eyebrow fell off. And he never bothered to have another grafted on. But the accident didn't dampen Earl's spirit nor end his flying career. After World War I, and also in World War II he had great success with gliders and he also worked with the Link Trainer which taught the essentials of flying from a simulated airplane cockpit.

Paul's anxiety over Earl as he pulled him from the wreck that day was overwhelming. He was sure Earl had been killed for who could survive such a crash. But after checking at the hospital across the street, and being reassured that everything possible was being done for Earl and his student, he returned to the field, and to his job. He took comfort in the knowledge that the Chief Surgeon at the hospital was a colleague of my father's in the American College of Surgeons and Dad had spoken highly of his ability and skill. We knew he would pull them through if anyone could. And of course he did, and Earl lived to be 75 years old.

Paul knew how important it was both for him and for his students to get right back into the saddle. He collected his students again at the acrobatic stage and even added Earl's woebegone class to his and gave them all a good lecture, and in no uncertain terms, (Paul was good at that), of what happens when a flyer freezes on the controls. They had seen for themselves first hand! Then Paul took each student up for a short hop because he knew he must get them right back up in the air that very day lest they lose their nerve.

We knew well the splendid courage of those student aviators and we rejoiced with them when they made the grade and soloed successfully. But we also knew the heartbreak and disappointment of the ones who washed out. We too felt the grief of the pilots who lost their buddies when the inevitable crashes resulted in death. We loved those young student aviators and many became our lifelong friends. Many came to our quarters to say goodbye after graduation, proud of their wings, and of their overseas orders in their hands, and many kept in touch by letters sent to us from France.

From my strategic position at Quarters 58-A, it was inevitable that I should be aware of all of the activity going on around me. I saw airplanes collide in midair, lock horns and circle earthward. I turned away in horror with a prayer on my lips when a cloud of dust rising from the field told me my worst fears had been realized. Again, I saw airplanes struggling in the deadly clutches of the dreaded tailspin. The plane would come down in a sort of corkscrew turn, head down and tail circling in a wide arc. At that time a tailspin was almost always fatal unless the pilot had enough altitude when it fell into the spin to pull it out before it was too late. There was no foolproof way to take an airplane out of a tailspin in those days. It remained for Eddie Stinson, the fearless pioneer pilot, to experiment with the problem until he happened upon the solution. He gave this information to the aviation world and it proved to be a boon to flyers. Paul received a small booklet on the subject, tried out Eddie's theory and it worked. Eddie will be remembered as one of the three flying Stinsons, Eddie, Katherine and Marjory who made pioneer aviation history. Eddie was well known as the builder of the Stinson airplane, and for his part in the early development of aviation. His career was tragically cut short when the airplane in which he was flying to Chicago, hit a flag pole in Jackson Park as he was about to land and he was killed.

The saddest and most poignant moments for us were the times when the gray hearse came out from Houston, always at dusk or under cover of night, and pulled up at the back door of the hospital to bear its precious burden away. What tragedy, and what sadness for some American home.

It was just such happenings as these that convinced me that a change would be good for Paul as well as for me and that is why I welcomed the army orders which he received on May 1, 1918, ordering him to "proceed" to Mineola, Long Island, New York.

Could it be that these orders were not actually for the Air Mail Service after all, Paul reasoned. They did not specify any such duty. But the rumor around Ellington was that plans for an Air Mail experiment were in the works and that several Army aviators were to be lent to the Post Office Department to do the flying. There was encouragement in being ordered to Mineola however, and Paul held out a glimmer of hope that now at long last, he might be on his way to overseas duty. He thought so because once before in the spring of 1917, he had received similar orders and had reported there and made all preparations to go to France with the First Aero Squadron with Major Billy Mitchell in charge. In that group gathered there were Paul's old friends William "Bill" Schauffler, William Rolfe, Harold "Buck" Gallop and Walter Barnaby with whom he had trained in the Officers Reserve Corps of the Aviation Section of the Signal Corps, when it was first organized in 1916. In fact, they were the first five aviators selected for this training program when it was offered at the Curtiss Aviation School at Newport News, Virginia. He was glad to be reunited with these former buddies. But as it turned out, it was to be only a brief reunion.

There was no separate Army Air Corps in the beginning. Army aviation was developed in the Signal Corps, and it did not become a separate service until Congress passed the Overman Act on May 14, 1918. President Wilson approved it on May 20, and on that date the Air Service was officially separated from the Signal Corps. The President appointed Major General William L. Kenly (not an aviator) Director of Military Aeronautics; Air Service Aeronautics U.S. Army, and from that nucleus grew the present imposing Air Force.

Among the first Signal Corps officers who became interested in aviation was Major "Billy" Mitchell. Because there was no flying field in Washington in 1916, he along with Major Tom Milling and other Signal Corps officers often came down to the Curtiss school to take flying lessons. They would take the night boat to Old Point Comfort, stay at the old Chamberlin Hotel where the Navy had such gay and colorful parties when the Fleet was in Hampton Roads, and when the Navy wives joined their husbands for a gala reunion. Then they would arrive at the Curtiss school on Saturdays for dual instructions with Jimmy Johnson, Walter Lees and any other flight instructor who was available. Major Mitchell had already had some dual instruction, in fact he never passed up an opportunity to take a hop anywhere there was an airplane available, but he was eager to take the regular pilot training course, fly solo and get his official pilots license.

His weekend visits were always welcome because he would bring us the latest news from Washington. He was convinced, even at that time, of the importance of military aviation in spite of the fact that many of his fellow officers and many Congressmen disagreed with him. They thought it was of little value and that Billy Mitchell was too impractical, impetuous and visionary. From the very beginning he was the champion of military aviation and was instrumental in setting up and promoting an aviation program and urging legislation to finance it.

It was mainly under his persistence that Congress passed a bill in the late fall of 1916 providing the necessary appropriation to expand the aviation section of the Signal Corps, and to include a Reserve Officers Training Program. He brought this information to the group of young aviation students at Newport News and urged any who were interested to make application at once. He told them that the government was to finance the course and that the students were to receive the pay of Sergeants while in training and upon completion of the course were to be commissioned First Lieutenants in the Officers Reserve Corps of the Signal Corps. This looked like a good proposition, especially since everyone realized that war clouds were hanging low and they would need this military training soon.

A half dozen flyers, Paul among them, hurried up to Washington on November 15 to enlist in this program and to take the aptitude tests and the first examinations offered by this new course. The candidates were Schauffler, Rolfe, Barnaby, Gallop, Paul, and William Bouldin, and they considered themselves lucky to be the first to avail themselves of this opportunity even though it was so new that they were the guinea pigs for the project. The examining officers and medics seemed to just make up the tests as they went along for as yet, there was no established nor standard procedure. Naturally there was the usual complete physical to start with, followed by tests to determine their fitness to be military aviators. Paul afterward related how he was seated on a sort of revolving piano stool, whirled around and then checked for his reaction and reflexes. Next came the eye and color-blind tests. Then each one had to walk a chalk line to test his equilibrium. I listened to these candidates talk it over afterwards, hilariously recalling how funny it was, especially since they had been out on the town the night before!

Having been put through their paces they returned to Newport News to await the verdict. As they eagerly watched the daily mail for the answer they began to speculate on various things such as what sort of uniforms they would be required to wear and what their insignia would be. One alert New York firm had already submitted a design for a fancy special uniform for aviators, the distinguishing mark being silver wings embroidered on a black patch on the left breast pocket. As it developed this insignia was adopted, but there was to be no special uniform. The only distinguishing marks for aviators were the coveted wings on the pocket.The olive drab of "the brown shoe Army" became the standard except for the Knickerbocker type trousers which the aviation branch wore with wrap leggings or puttees for everyday wear, and for dress-up with high leather boots with spurs. The usual facetious reply to the query "whatever do aviators need spurs for?" was that only Kiwis (the Army term for non-flying officers) wore them, and that was the way they kept their feet from sliding off their desks!

December 9, 1916 was memorable because of the report which came from Washington that Culver, Barnaby, Schauffler, Rolfe and Gallup had passed the tests. They were sorry that Bill Bouldin's name was not on the list, but they were not surprised that he hadn't made it because of his physical condition. Bill was hobbling about with a cane at the time, while recovering from the effects of an airplane accident and actually he had not been equal to the tests at that time. However, later on when his injuries had healed, Bill obtained a commission in the U.S. Navy. We assumed Bill's family was not too enthusiastic over his interest in flying, especially because of his accident, and this was confirmed when after they were informed he had not passed the Signal Corps test they telegraphed this reply: "Congratulations, now come home and tend to business."

After these five original Reserve officers of the Aviation Section of the Signal Corps finished their training course in the spring of 1917, they were to be separated by the call to arms and never to meet again. All five received orders for overseas duty with the First Aero Squadron. Bill Schauffler became a member of General Mitchell's staff in France and flew many missions in World War I. In World War II he was Colonel W.G. Schauffler in charge of Geiger Field in the state of Washington. He passed away in 1951, a victim of pneumonia. Walter Barnaby was shot down in combat over France in the early part of the war and was so seriously wounded that he died shortly after, but not before being awarded the Croix de Guerre. We lost track of Bill Rolfe; but we were to learn that Buck Gallop became Commander of the 90th Aero Squadron in France and that he had been seriously wounded. After the war he was awarded the Croix de Guerre with Palms, for bravery in action at St. Mihiel and the Argonne Meuse drive, at a special ceremony before a review of the entire command at Langley Field, Virginia.

Paul was separated from this group by a strange turn of fate, as they were preparing to sail from New York in the spring of 1917 when last minute orders from the War Department ordered him to report at once to Princeton University.

2
Princeton

When it seemed inevitable that the United States would be drawn into the war, several colleges and universities began to expand their R.O.T.C. programs and to add other military training classes to their curriculum, and Princeton was one of the first to initiate an aviation training program. Many patriotic alumni, inspired by the leadershp of the famous author and war correspondent Major James Barnes of the class of 1891, and including Percy Pyne of the class of 1879, and Marshall Mills of the class of 1902, and many others contributed and collected funds for the establishment of an aviation training school as part of Princeton's preparedness program in the spring of 1917. They selected a site about three miles out of town on the Lawrenceville Road, had a strip cleared on an adjacent small farm to use as a landing field, erected a wooden hangar and a small lunch-room and club house, installed four training planes, and hired several aviation mechanics and flying instructors. This was the Princeton Flying School. Civilian pilot Frank Stanton, and Lieutenant E.R. Kenneson were already on duty when Paul arrived with his War Department orders. Thirty-eight students had already applied for flying lessons and applications for instruction were pouring in. The alumni realized that with graduation in June there would be still more. That was why Princeton called on Washington for another instructor and Paul was the one chosen, and that is why he went to Princeton and not to France.

Upon arriving Paul was greeted by Major Barnes who handed him a letter which stated in writing what his official duties were. It said in part that he was to be "commandant of the flying field with jurisdiction over the mechanics and watchmen, and have general supervision of flying." He found that he was not only to shoulder that responsibiltity but he was to teach flying and also set up a ground school on the Princeton campus.

Princeton's patriotic gesture in establishing a flying school before war was declared made it a natural selection for one of the government's first ground schools. This consisted of an eight week course of training in the mechanics of aviation and tactics of military flying. The University offered Patton Hall for this purpose, its study halls for classrooms and the campus for a drill ground. These facilities were at Paul's disposal as he struggled with his two-fold duty — quite an assignment for a young man of twenty-four years. But he knew how to fly and the Princeton lads were apt pupils, and he knew the mechanics of the airplane, having worked in the shop at the Curtiss Flying School. And he had some knowledge of military aeronautics from his Signal Corps training and something about Army regulations from his schooling at St. Johns Military Academy at Delafield, Wisconsin, but how was he to coordinate all of this? He had no choice but to plunge in. So he called all the aviation students together and briefed them on what the plans were and told them about the outlines and suggestions that had come from Washington. The curriculum included military drill — which Paul was already familiar with — but this was his first experience at organization. So after calling for volunteers who had similar training, he found that one of the students, Paul Nelson, had been to Culver Military Academy and that two or three others had been to summer encampment at Plattsburg, so they were familiar with the military. They became an invaluable help. Then he learned that the Princeton students had organized their own military drill the previous winter, and so before long all the aviation students were added to this group, doing "squads right and squads left" on the campus. The classes in mechanics were soon coordinated with flying lessons and the ground school was off to a good start.

At this point Paul had reason to be grateful for his Prep school training, and that brought to mind a letter he had received (and which I still have) from Sidney T. Smythe, Headmaster of St. Johns, in 1916. It was his reply to Paul's letter asking for a recommendation to the Signal Corps. It said "I am pleased to recommend you to the Aviation Section of the Signal Corps but I cannot for the life of me understand what your wife is thinking of, letting you go into this flying business — unless she wants to get rid of you which I hope she does not." What would Dr. Smythe say now that aviation was coming into its own, Paul wondered. He would at least be pleased to know that one of his former students was putting his military knowledge to practical use in the war effort.

Paul divided his time between the flying field and the Princeton campus. He much preferred the former, especially after an avalanche of orders and directions poured in from Washington swamping him and his staff. But the ground school was going strong by the time Major Benjamin Foulois, who was in charge of all newly established ground schools, got around to visit Princeton. Paul had done his best to bring order out of chaos, to set up classes and equip machine shops, and I believe the Major was pleased with what he found.

The military was in evidence everywhere. The drilling on Poe Memorial Field every afternoon and the sputtering whirr of airplane engines overhead, or on the test blocks, became familiar sights and sounds to the Princeton residents as well as a constant reminder of the coming war. Major Foulois must have been both surprised and grateful that the amateurs had carried on so well while waiting for his expert advice and instructions. No one knew more about aviation and its challenges than Benjamin Foulois for he had been part of it from the beginning. He had taught himself to fly after brief instruction from both Wilbur and Orville Wright and made aviation his career. The next time I was to see Major Foulois was many years after when as a retired Major General he appeared on the TV show "I've Got a Secret." His secret was that "he *was* the Army Air Force in 1909." He went on the relate some interesting experiences of his early flying days and his verdict on current aviation left no doubt that he preferred the good old days when he remarked "jet flying is monotonous as hell. They've taken all the fun out of flying." Major General Foulois passed away in April 1967 at the age of 87 after a brilliant life-long career in aviation.

Meanwhile, Paul and I had arrived at Princeton several weeks before commencement week in 1917 and established ourselves in the lovely old Nassau Inn across the street from the University campus. I wonder if it had ever occured to Woodrow Wilson when he was a college professor there and later its President, that he was a man of destiny who would one day, as President of the United States, have the enormous responsibility of leading his country in a terrible world war, which was supposed to end all wars and establish and insure universal peace and brotherhood.

A strange nostalgia came over me as I listened to the "sings" on campus across the street or to the melodious strains which floated up from the basement tap room of the Nassau Inn in the evenings when the seniors, clad in their traditional white overall suits (they called this uniform their drinking suits) would congregate to sing their old college songs and to carve their initials on the heavy wooden topped tables, registering there so to speak, even as they engraved happy memories on their hearts, before leaving their beloved haunts to scatter to the four winds. Could it be that a whole year had gone by since I too had been going through all the exciting experiences of college graduation? The Hill at the University of Wisconsin seemed a long way off.

The Inn was filled with alumni — proud parents and families of the 1917 graduating class. It was a happy group, but there was also a certain restraint about the festivities because of the obvious preparations for war on all sides. I wondered how many future college commencement exercises would be held under war clouds? I still wonder that in 1985.

Before the government took over the Princeton Flying School and officially absorbed it at the outset of the war, I was allowed to have a flight with the permission of Mr. Mills, in one of the school's training planes with my husband as pilot. The students stood around watching curiously while Paul strapped me into the front seat of the open cockpit Curtiss Jenny. Before he climbed into the instructor's seat behind me, he leaned over and kissed me. In surprise at this sudden gesture I gulped: "Is this goodby forever?" to which Paul replied with a nonchalant wave to the amused audience "Oh, I always kiss my lady passengers!" With a flourish he swung into the seat behind me, both of us adjusted our goggles and he indicated he was all set. He signaled the mechanic to spin the prop, taxied to the end of the field, gave it the gun and in a moment we were off the ground flying into that "sweet, delicate, ethereal, gentle world" which the great French poet aviator Saint-Exupéry was one day to describe so beautifully.

My thoughts were filled with just such idyllic impressions, but I also kept thinking about the two attractive Broadway actresses, one being

Emma Haig of the Ziegfeld Follies, who stood in the crowd watching our take-off. They had come up from New York as guests of the two Princeton lads who had driven them out to the flying field in their Stutz Bearcat Roadster to arrange a flight for them. They were to be Paul's next passengers!

Another incident of Paul's Princeton duty in the interval before Uncle Sam took over was the unique experience of doubling for the hero in a movie called "The Lone Wolf" in which he did the flying sequences for the hero of the film. A movie company had arranged to have the stars Bert Lytell and Hazel Dawn come to Princeton for certain airplane episodes of the picture which were supposed to be shot on location. Paul was selected to double for Bert Lytell, not only in the flying scenes but in some of the long shots on the ground. We saw this movie some years later at our local movie theater and only we knew that in reality the hero was not Bert Lytell at all, but Paul Culver.

Several other persons took advantage of the use of the Princeton airplanes on the off-hours when the flying instructors were available, and such a one was James T. Hare, better known as Jimmy Hare, the veteran photographer for Colliers Magazine. He arranged for Paul to fly him around the New Jersey countryside taking birdseye pictures. He especially wanted to fly over Trenton so he could get an aerial picture of the area where Washington had crossed the Delaware many years before. Today, General Washington could have had airplane cover for that perilous crossing! When they returned, he took pictures of the Princeton flying field from the air and on the ground where he lined up the flyers for a group picture to use for an illustrated story that appeared in Leslie's Magazine August 16, 1917, describing Princeton's war preparations.

This was by no means Jimmy Hare's first aerial photography experience, for he related some hair raising tales of his earlier experiences in the air, such as the one during the Boer War in South Africa. He was allowed to go up in an observation balloon with two British officers to snap pictures from aloft while the battle raged below. Bullets rained around them, fortunately missing their mark. Regardless of the danger, Jimmy got some rare aerial pictures. He photographed many of the pioneer events of aviation, starting with Kitty Hawk. The Wright brothers had banned all picture taking at the North Carolina sand dunes when they had resumed flying tests there in 1908, just five years after their first successful flights. These new trials were test flights made in preparation for demonstrating their airplane to the Army at Washington, and also for certain commitments abroad. *Colliers Magazine* got word of this and sent Jimmy Hare and another reporter down to get pictures and a story. In spite of the prohibition of photographers, Jimmy succeeded in getting two long distance shots of the Wright airplane in the air from his concealed hiding place in a clump of bushes. Jimmy said that the sight of the two Wrights working there on the bleak sand dunes, and then actually flying, was an unforgettable picture. It was his story with its illustrations that was a scoop for Colliers.

Everyone knew the name of Jimmy Hare in those days, much as they did Huntley and Brinkley or Lowell Thomas for he chronicled the happenings of the day in the most graphic medium of those times — namely with pictures which he took on the spot. His war photography career began in 1898 when the Maine was blown up in the Havana Harbor. Here was a real scoop for any photographer! The ship blew up, and Jimmy Hare blew in and Robert Collier of Colliers Magazine commented that "Both were major explosions." He plunged in fearlessly, where the action was — in the Spanish American War; the Russo-Japanese War; the Boer War and World War I. He had survived every conceivable danger, weathered natural and unnatural catastrophies, oblivious to all else except a good camera account of it, so when Paul flew him at Princeton, he looped the loop, side-slipped and skimmed tree tops so he could get unusual angle shots, he knew that it was O.K. with Jimmy. As long as his camera was working, he was in his element. Not all passengers were that easy to please.

The finest thing that happened to us at Princeton was the birth of our first child, Paul Dodd Culver, born on June 28, 1917. Strangely enough he wasn't born with wings! But many years later he did earn his wings as a Navy pilot in World War II. He graduated from Pensacola the day before Pearl Harbor and was one of the first Navy pilots sent to the

Pacific Zone where he was to learn more about flying than his father ever knew. Then after twenty years of active duty in the United States Navy Air Corps, and having attained the rank of Commander, he retired to try his hand in business as a civilian.

All in all, the Princeton interlude was a happy and interesting experience. Paul enjoyed his association with his students, among whom were Harvey Firestone, Jr., Paul Robinson, Elliot White Springs, and the two Morgan boys from California whose petite and beautiful mother had been one of Paul's first women passengers. All of the young men took their training seriously and the flying field became the most popular part of the University.

Paul felt that he was getting good results at the flying field and at the ground school especially after having had nothing to start with but a lot of native courage, a mountain of government directives and endless paper work. He was doing the best he could, even if this duty had deprived him of sailing to France with his buddies. So when government orders #163, dated July 16, 1917 were handed to him, he tore open the envelope expectantly thinking that at long last, these were his overseas orders. But no such luck. He was again to have stateside duty, this time at Wilbur Wright Field, near Dayton, Ohio where the largest army aviation school ever built in this country was nearing completion. The importance of his new duty should have offset Paul's disappointment for he was not only to be a flying instructor there, but a field engineer as well, and he would have no more ground school responsibility. That was a relief.

3
Dayton

There was magic in the very name Dayton — the city that gave the Wright brothers to the world. Our move to that area was to prove as interesting as the previous city, although we were to find ourselves under stricter regulations after war was declared. Wilbur Wright Field was located at Fairfield, Ohio, a village a few miles out of Dayton. Under construction were two huge flying fields with mile long runways, dozens of hangars, barracks, ground school buildings, shops, recreation building, hospital, the PX and row upon row of officers' quarters and a fine big house for the commanding officer, Major Arthur Christie. It was a beehive of activity as the war effort speeded up and it was one of the first complete aviation training centers which were springing up all over the country. We had never seen anything like it. It seemed aviation had suddenly come of age, spurred on by the war emergency.

The officers' quarters were not yet finished so we stayed in Dayton at the Miami Hotel until they were ready. The Miami was already a virtual officers club as aviators and engineers gathered there, and newspaper reporters and photographers swarmed into the lobby to greet the incoming aviation crowd and to get stories and pictures. This time the newspapers would not pass up a scoop, as they had done on December 17, 1903. On that day Bishop Milton Wright had stopped at the newspaper office in Dayton to report a telegram he had just received from his sons, Wilbur and Orville, at Kitty Hawk, North Carolina, stating they had made a successful powered flight. But the newspaper didn't even bother to print the item. Here was an example of the Biblical phrase from Matthew 13, Verse 5, that "a prophet is not without honor, save in his own country and in his own house." But the latter part of the quote does not fit this case because Wilbur and Orville Wright did have the confidence of their own family and even financial assistance, especially from their school teacher sister, Katharine.

The townspeople knew that the Wright boys were tinkering with kites and gliders and engines, but powered flight was an idea too fantastic to be believed, much less to be chronicled. And so the world-shaking event of December 17, 1903 went unheralded and unnoticed by the Dayton newspapers and the other papers across the land — except two that I know of: "The Virginia Pilot" of Norfolk, Virginia and the "Cincinnati Inquirer." Both gave it brief mention.

However, this time the Dayton papers were not going to pass up a good story, but were determined to do full justice to this aviation event. We felt the papers had overdone it in the coverage they gave the aviators because by 1917 aviation was a familiar story around Dayton, but the arrival of so many airmen, servicemen as well as civilian flyers, created a stir and the town was agog over the surge of war activity in its midst. The Dayton Sunday News of July 29, 1917 carried a feature story on some of the aviators, using their pictures and biographical sketch of each one under the heading "Face to Face With Real Men." Paul was one of them. There was Major Arthur Christie, Commandant of the Wilbur Wright Field, Captain Maxwell Kirby, Captain J.B. McCauley, Captain C.S. Jackson, and Victor Vernon, Chief Civilian Instructor, to mention a few. Several French and Canadian flyers who had come to Dayton in advisory capacity were pictured, among them Canada's leading Ace pilot General William Bishop, who had brought down 72 German planes single-handed. What a handsome, boyish, blond young man he was, to be called a veteran war pilot, and to have won so many citations. He wore decorations for bravery awarded by England, Canada and France. He even wore the Victoria Cross, an honor granted to few airmen up to that time. Now he was taking time out from combat duty to visit American flying schools to spark their activity.

Dayton welcomed all these newcomers with open arms and an enthusiasm which was so genuine and hearty that I, for one, was sorry when our quarters out at the Field were finished and ready for us to move into. As we drove out to the Field, we passed the Huffman prairie where not too many years before, the Wright brothers had tried out their kites and gliders. The very shed which had housed these in 1900 before they departed for their historic flight at Kitty Hawk, was still there. In fact, even the catapult they used to launch their gliders was still standing.

A few interested spectators used to come out to watch the experiments in the early days, and now in 1917, crowds began to line up around the adjacent Wilbur Wright Field to watch the modern version of flying. Everyone agreed it was well named "Wilbur Wright Field" even if that famous man would never know of the honor since he had passed away a few years before in 1912. But it served as a fitting memorial to him, as well as a reminder to the other members of the Wright family that the government remembered its debt to them.

We watched this Field grow as block after block of hangars, houses, barracks, and so on were completed and hundreds of men arrived daily to take up duty there.

When we reached the Field we realized more than ever that now we were at war. The entire area was surrounded by a high wire fence and we could enter the tightly guarded entrance gate only upon presenting official admission cards. Strict military rules and discipline were observed by everyone, civilian employees as well as the military.

The air seemed literally full of airplanes, a strange new experience for us. Up to a short time ago the sight of more than one or two airplanes aloft at once was a rare occurance. Flying schools and training centers were springing up all over the nation and this one near Dayton, the first complete aviation training center to go into operation, was teeming with activity. All the instructors were busy from sun-up until dusk teaching pilots on the dual-control airplanes, supervising their solo flights and then sending them on to other stages to be trained as fighter pilots and bombadiers. As the need arose, civilian pilots were hired. Among them were Victor Vernon, Walter Lees, Ernest Hall, Ivan P. Wheaton, Earl Southee and many others. Their arrival was like old home week to us, for they were friends from the days when we were all together at the Curtiss School at Newport News, Virginia. We were also to greet friends from our former Princeton days when some of Paul's students, such as Harvey Firestone, Jr. and Paul Robinson, who having completed their ground school and preliminary flight training, came to Wilbur Wright for advanced flying courses.

We were assigned to regulation officer's quarters, four room cottages with screened porches and meager furnishings which we augmented with purchases from a furniture store in Dayton. And we rented a piano. Our little cottage had no central heat nor was it insulated, so it was necessary to stoke our one potbellied stove as well as the coal burning flat top cookstove continually against the bitter cold of that winter of record severity in 1917-18. We used to tack Army blankets across the windows to keep out cold winds that had a wide sweep across the flying field toward the long row of officer's quarters. Paul and his brother, Sergeant Miller Culver who was staying with us at the time, often took turns sitting up all night stoking the fires.

No wonder that when official orders reached Paul shortly before Christmas 1917 (and they were for Ellington Field, Houston, Texas), they were more than orders — they were welcome release from the cold weather. We were soon on a warm train bound for Houston along with a crowd of other service people, also glad to be leaving the bitter cold of the frozen north.

But we left behind memories of a good job well done. Paul relished his Dayton duty, his part in the supervision of maintenance of the airplanes as an engineering officer and in the pilot training program. He had turned out many finished pilots and was grateful that none of his students had had a fatal accident. There were crack-ups, wash-outs and problem students, but the output of flyers had been gratifying and he looked forward to similar success at Ellington Field.

4
Houston

It seemed we were destined to arrive at every Post before they were ready for us. We spent a few days at the Rice Hotel in Houston before moving out to Ellington Field. Pioneer aviation was booming around Houston that winter, even though only 13 years had elapsed since the Wright brothers' first flights. Now after decades there is still a pioneer aviation activity in Houston, except that the NASA activity there is so very different. For we have moved into the space age currently and have seen man walking on the moon. If any of our contemporaries had ventured any such prediction he would have been eyed with suspicion.

Speaking of predictions: little did we then dream that by the time our small son who accompanied us to Houston, had grown up, there would be a second world war, which he would take part in, and that after the war he would be Air Operations Officer on the aircraft carrier Oriskany and that one of his top notch pilots in the all weather fighter squadron was a young Navy Lieutenant named Alan B. Shepard, Jr. who was destined to be America's first astronaut to be rocketed into the stratosphere. Nor looking further into the future could we have predicted that two more children would join our little family circle in the next ten years to also take part in World War II. John to be a Navy Aircrewman; and Edith to serve as a volunteer driver in the Signal corps. Later, being determined not to be outdone by her father and two brothers, she too learned to fly.

Houston was gayly decorated for the holidays when we arrived, but its wreaths and tinsel without the atmosphere of cold and snow seemed out of place to us who were accustomed to a white Christmas in Wisconsin. As we drove out to Ellington, the flat treeless plains that rolled out before us during the fifteen or so mile trip suggested anything but the traditional holiday song: "Over the river and through the woods" and moreover it was as warm as summer. Upon arriving at our quarters 58-A, we found ourselves in the center of a huge complex of buildings that paralleled long lines of hangars stretching as far as we could see. Our quarters were identical to the ones at Wilbur Wright so we should have felt at home immediately. And they too were only partially furnished. There was a round golden oak dining table and four matching chairs, three metal army cots minus mattresses and a small coal stove. After surveying the equipment, Paul suggested I go back to town and stay at the hotel until our furniture arrived. Had he forgotten that his wife was a pioneer at heart? Wasn't this much better than the creature comforts pioneer American wives endured when they willingly followed their men into wilderness in the winning of the west? I have always had deep respect for the very word Pioneer. To me it means much more than Webster's definition which says in part: "One who goes before preparing the way for others." My admiration for pioneers began in childhood because I had been born and reared to that life as the daughter of a pioneer surgeon who had braved the wild rough lumbering area of Northern Wisconsin in the 1890's. And now I was the wife of a pioneer aviator who was a member of the Early Birds of Aviation. Certainly I would not weaken now and go back to town.

Paul went out to forage around to see what he could buy or requisition and came back with his arms full of olive-drab army blankets and a carton of canned goods from the canteen. Someone sent over a "striker," an enlisted man who would do odd jobs whenever he had time off from regular duty. Our man, named Osborn, was pure gold. He even became our baby sitter. He helped us pad the springs of our metal cots with newspapers and folded blankets. Next morning Paul and I looked like waffles with the pattern of the springs deeply etched in our flesh. Otherwise we were comfortable and set to enjoy the holidays.

Then we began to unpack our few belongings and try to get the Christmas spirit for we were to celebrate our baby son's first Christmas. Being strangers in a strange land and accustomed to family gatherings at Christmas time, we admitted we were homesick. So we were delighted when we received an invitation from the Commanding Officer John Curry to have a Christmas dinner and spend the day along with all the other new families at the officer's club. There we met congenial friends and thanks to them, the holiday season was a happy one.

With the start of 1918 Paul was hard at work teaching flying on the acrobatic stage as well as attending to his duties as Commanding Officer of the 189th Aero Squadron and it was there at Ellington that he received his orders that he was to proceed at once to Mineola, Long Island. He began to wind up his classes on the advanced flying stage and we packed our belongings to leave for New York. Many of his students came to say goodbye — and some to even thank him for being the tough instructor he was reputed to be. He hadn't lost one student. Men from his squadron also dropped in and we realized we were reluctant to leave these good friends. Everyone helped us pack, especially our dear friends Evelyn and Bill Mulvihill who were sharing our quarters at the time.

To come was Bill's tragic death in the fall of 1918 at an airfield in Florida and it seemed doubly unnecessary because it happened right after the Armistice was signed. Diving his airplane at an aerial target, it became entangled in the rigging and caused him to crash. His distraught young widow and baby daughter made the sad journey back to Pittsburgh with Bill's body, and Paul accompanied them to perform the unhappy duty of being a pall bearer.

Meanwhile, in happier times, the Mulvihills drove us into Houston and put us on the New York train along with hundreds of other service people all bound for New York and overseas, and Paul hoped that he was too and that finally his dream about going to France was to come true. It seemed like a long, slow journey and the train was crowded to capacity, but our baby son Paul kept us busy and occupied. It was never a problem for us to find a baby sitter when Paul and I went to the diner. Baby Paul was so friendly and good natured they began to call him Jim Dandy, and Sunny Jim, and from that came his nickname "Jim" which has clung to him ever since.

5
First Aerial Mail

Paul's orders directed him to report to Major E.L. Canady, commanding Officer of Hazelhurst Aviation Field at Mineola. Major Canady received him at once and handed him his latest orders which assigned him to his duties with the aerial mail service.

He wasn't to be sent overseas after all! He reasoned to himself as he made his way back to the hotel to break the news to me: "what in the world is the government thinking of, taking pilots and airplanes, so badly needed here and overseas, for an air mail route? Why, we've got a war on our hands, let's win that first! Can you feature being a mailman when there is a war on, especially after putting in hundreds of hours training students in combat flying to help win the war. Why can't the railroads carry the mail the way they've always done?" We knew that Earl Ovington out in California had gotten permission from the Post Office Department to fly sacks of mail between certain points out there for a short period to show that it could be done, but President Wilson's project was an entirely different matter. Air mail could never measure up to the slogan which was the official motto of the National Association of Letter Carriers, engraved on the facade of the General Post Office in New York City which reads: "Neither snow nor rain nor heat nor gloom of night stays these couriers from the swift completion of their appointed rounds." Maybe it was true at ground level but it was too much to expect of an aerial postal service. Then he remarked "when my children shall ask me what brave deeds I did in World War I and I have to tell them I just carried air mail, they won't think that took much courage."

But it did no good, for in the service orders are orders. However he was soon to change his attitude after he learned the purpose of the air mail service: that it was designed to speed up the war effort by flying important mail between Washington, Philadelphia and New York; and to give pilots practice in flying mail cross country. The War Department was even then looking ahead to the end of the war and to the extension of air mail routes. This would insure post-war employment for the oversupply of both airplanes, pilots and mechanics which the war had necessitated; and also that by constant practice pilots would be ready for any future military emergency. This sounded reasonable.

But my reaction to Paul's air mail assignment was quite different. I understood his frustration and disappointment over not going overseas, at least not yet, and I was glad because it pushed that separation day a bit farther back. Then too, I considered it a real honor that Paul should be chosen as one of the pilots to inaugurate this important air mail service. But nothing I could say helped. He was downcast. That is, until he met the rest of the crew.

Here were kindred spirits, men he knew he would enjoy working with. How else would Paul ever have known such men as Major Reuben Fleet, and Lieutenants: Torrey Webb, Jim Edgerton, Steve Bonsal, George Boyle and Walter Miller? If they could take it, he certainly could.

Major Fleet was in charge of the entire project and the other pilots were soon to know why. His dynamic personality and enthusiasm were contagious and things began to happen immediately. Years later, in fact during the fortieth anniversary of the start of the air mail service, Paul was to write to Reuben Fleet: "I recall with pleasure the privilege of having been associated with you in the historic air mail venture and the great kick I got out of your enthusiasm and your bustling activity. I knew right then that I was working with a personality who was really going to make things happen, or blow his top in the attempt."

President Wilson had been discussing the idea of air mail service with his Cabinet and the Post Office Department since early spring and an agreement was reached on March 1, 1918, to operate an air mail service jointly with the Post Office Department, and the Congress appropriated $100,000 for it. But the officers in the Air Service, who were to be charged with the responsibility of organizing it knew nothing about this until the orders of May 3, 1918, and the pilots who were to fly it, got even shorter notice.

Quoting from a speech which Major Fleet, the Air Mail Number One pilot, made before the Air Mail Pilots Convention at Reno on October 15, 1966: "On Friday, 3 May 1918, the War Department issued an order to its Air Service Aeronautics to inaugurate an Aerial Mail Service between Washington and New York each way every day except Sunday, to depart both terminals at 11:00 a.m., beginning Wednesday, 15 May 1918, with intermediate landing and mail service at Philadelphia by both north and south bound airplanes. Airline distance between north and south terminals — 218 miles. The order was issued by Newton D. Baker, the Secretary of War, at the request of the Post Officer Department, under direction of Woodrow Wilson, the President of the United States. A.S. Burleson was the Postmaster General; Otto Praeger, Second Assistant Postmaster General was in charge of transportation of all mail. Never before had mail been carried in the world by air at an announced time to and from designated places on a schedule operation irrespective of weather."

Upon recommendation of Colonel H.H. "Hap" Arnold, Major Fleet was to be in complete charge of the Aerial Mail Service. The powers-that-be knew where to look for the man who could carry out the order on such short notice. It takes a busy man to get things done. Major Fleet J.M.A., A.S.A., U.S.A. was Executive Officer for Flying Training in the United States stationed at the Air Service Signal Corps Headquarters with thirty-four flying fields under his command. When the responsibility of the aerial mail was added to his already full schedule, he was called to the White House to confer with Secretary of War Baker and Postmaster General Burleson on May 6th to go over the plans. Major Fleet reported that the Air Service had no airplanes capable of flying non-stop from Washington to Philadelphia or from Philadelphia to New York, and he requested postponement to gain more time than the allotted eight days, in order to secure several Curtiss NJ6H airplanes and to adapt them to the mail service.

To continue Reuben Fleet's quote: "Secretary Baker invited Secretary Burleson to his office; Burleson went into a rage over the suggestion for deferment, stating he had already announced to the Press that an Army Aerial Mail Service would get started on 15 May, and that it had to start then, even if war work suffered. Secretary Baker was sympathetic with my recommendation but the fact that the Press had been advised that the Aerial Mail Service would start on 15 May was governing, and the War Department had to do it even if its aviators had to land in meadows enroute and retank with gasoline, oil and maybe water."

"Without leaving Secretary Baker's officer, I telephoned Colonel E.A. Deeds, A.S.P. (Air Service Production), and requested him to order six JN6Hs from Curtiss Aeroplane and Motor Corporation at Garden City, Long Island, New York, which firm was manufacturing trainers for the Army, leaving out the front seat and the front control, and substituting in the front cockpit a hopper to carry mail; also installing in each airplane, double capacity for gasoline and oil; the six airplanes to be delivered to us at Mineola Air Field in eight days."

"Curtiss accepted the telephoned order and agreed to have ready the six such airplanes at the sacrifice of suspending delivery of Army trainers during this period. They proposed to use two regular nineteen gallon gasoline tanks and two regular two-and-one-half gallon oil tanks, hooking together each pair of tanks to double the fuel capacity. The normal range of a Curtiss JN6H airplane trainer with a gasoline tank carrying 19 gallons was 88 miles in one hour and twenty minutes, at cruising speed of 66 miles an hour, reduced by head-winds and accelerated by tail winds. They were powered by 150 H.P. Hispano-Suiza motors and capable of carrying a 300 pound load.

Having arranged for the planes, the next step was to find suitable landing fields at the three terminal points. Through his friendship with Major August Belmont, Major Fleet was able to secure the use of of his park, the Belmont Race Track on Long Island, as the New York terminus for the Air Mail. There was a flying field nearby at Mineola, but the Army did not want the Air Mail to land there and interrupt its training program; so having decided on Belmont Park, a hangar was hastily constructed and a corps of mechanics brought over from Mineola to service the planes that were to carry the mail. The race track was in good condition for landing airplanes and it was also large enough so the huge grandstand there was not a serious hazard, nor had it been when on this very race track an international aviation meet had been held in 1910, in which such famous pioneers as Graham-White, Brookins, Moisant, Latham and

Glenn Curtiss had participated. There was great activity everywhere and everyone was wondering if the airplanes would be ready on time. Those were tense and anxious days.

At Philadelphia, the intermediate terminal, a field was selected on the advice of the Postmaster there on the Lincoln Highway about 12 miles outside the city near the village of Bustleton. From this point the mail could be quickly dispatched into Philadelphia by truck. Two sheet metal hangars and a small building which served as Post Office, were quickly erected, gas pumps installed and a corps of airplane mechanics and a postal clerk were installed. The adjoining farmer's field was leveled off for landing. It had a grass surface, and was adequate in size and smooth enough for any airplane to land on.

There being no flying field in Washington at that time, the Polo Field in Potomac Park was selected as the Southern terminal. Similar equipment was installed there and preparation for the big day went on.

That was the set-up Major Fleet described to his air mail pilots when they met at Mineola to be briefed on their new duty and to be warned there wasn't a minute to spare if the air mail was to start on time. With the Press already printing the story, they could not turn back now. By hook or crook, the air mail must start on May 15th even against Major Fleet's better judgement. But he knew he could count on his pilots, since he had selected most of them himself.

Each wondered why he had been selected, but was glad to be reassured that he was only on temporary loan to the Post Office Department and that eventually he would be returned to the Army. Paul learned that Major Fleet had selected him because of his good record as an Army aviator, his previous experience as a test pilot at Curtiss Aviation School at Newport News, and his training in the aviation section of the Signal Corps and at Princeton.

One of the pilots, Lieutenant Torrey Webb had completed his aviation training at Ellington Field which brought him to Major Fleet's attention. He had enlisted in the Air Service after graduating from Columbia and was headed for a career as a mining engineer but he went into oil instead and in the years following the war, he eventually became a vice president of Texas Oil Company before he retired.

Another pilot, Second Lieutenant Stephen Bonsal was the son of the famous war correspondent for whom he was named. He sought his adventure in the Army Air Service rather than in journalism after graduating from Yale.

We did not get to know Lieutenant Walter Miller as well nor did we know his background; but Paul used to tell how Lieutenant Miller reported for duty with a revolver tucked in his belt, saying no one would tamper with Uncle Sam's mail while he was entrusted with it.

Later, we learned from Major Fleet why Lieutenants Edgerton and Boyle had been selected. To quote Major Fleet again: "I had personally selected and detailed for the Aerial Mail Service, R.M.A.'s First Lieutenants Howard Paul Culver, Torrey H. Webb, and Walter Miller, and Second Lieutenant Stephen Bonsal and the Post Office Department had requested that Second Lieutenants James Clark Edgerton and George Leroy Boyle be detailed by us for the Aerial Mail Service. Edgerton's father was purchasing agent for the Post Office Department; Lieutenant Edgerton had just graduated from primary instruction as an aviator at Ellington Field. Lieutenant Boyle's father-in-law (to be) was Judge Charles C. McChord, Interstate Commerce Commissioner who had "Saved the parcel post for the Post Office Department" against private express companies bidding and fighting in court for the business. The Post Office Department requested that Lieutenant Boyle fly the first aerial mail from Washington, and Lieutenant Edgerton into Washington."

Meanwhile, I feel I had a part in the first aerial mail venture because I was so close to it. I kept a daily diary, and I subscribed to the Hemstreet Press clipping bureau in New York because all the Eastern papers gave so much space to this historic event. I collected and saved all the air mail data and mementos I could. Paul couldn't understand why I kept "all that stuff," but years later when I assembled the clippings and notices into a scrapbook and entitled it "First Aerial Mail" and gave it to him as a surprise birthday present, he was both surprised and pleased. I had this Latin phrase inscribed on the cover of the scrapbook: "Haec olim meminisse juvabit" which translated means something like: "Some day you will be glad to remember these things." These words, which were inscribed in the tiles over the fireplace in my Gamma Phi Beta Sorority House at the University of Wisconsin, had made an indelible impression on me, and they seemed to fit the occasion on Paul's thirty-fifth birthday. That book is now at the Smithsonian in Washington.

I watched from the side lines at the New York Terminal as preparations went forward to inaugurate the aerial mail service. They called it "Aerial Mail" at first and later just plain Air Mail. Through the courtesy of August Belmont, Paul and I were invited to live in the Turf and Field Club House located near the Belmont Park race track. We had a beautiful bedroom and also the use of the parlors and dining room and all the services. Each day when I would take my small son out for an airing and stroll through the lovely grounds, I would go over to the race track to watch the progress on the hangar and the other preparations for the big day. I couldn't see how they could possibly be ready by the 15th.

On May 13th, Major Fleet took all five of the aerial mail pilots except Lieutenant Boyle, who was in Washington, over to the Curtiss factory at Garden City to check on the mail planes. Paul told me how they all pitched in and worked through the night and into the next day helping the mechanics and engineers, so that by the afternoon of the 14th at least two of the air mail planes were flyable. To again quote from Reuben Fleet's 1966 speech before the Air Mail Pioneers: "I left Lieutenant Webb in charge at Belmont Park and the Curtiss plant, with Lieutenant Miller and Bonsal helping, and in reserve, and instructed Webb to get the other four aerial mail airplanes ready, and fly one from Belmont Park with the aerial mail at eleven the next morning to Bustleton Field, which the Philadelphia Postmaster had selected for Philadelphia. Edgerton at Bustelton Field would relieve Lieutenant Webb there and fly on to Washington, while Lieutenant Culver would relay the aerial mail at Bustleton to Belmont Park in New York."

The next move was the transportation of the other pilots to their designated postions. On the afternoon of the 14th, Major Fleet ordered Culver in No. 38262 and Edgerton in No. 38274 to take these two specially equipped aerial mail planes and fly them down to the

Philadelphia Field at Bustleton. Major Fleet went along in the third airplane which was a regular Curtiss JN4 training plane without extra fuel tanks. The weather was so foggy that none of the three pilots could see each other after take-off so it was almost a miracle that any of them managed to reach Philadelphia. At that time there were no airports, no improved instruments, no radio beam to bring the pilot into a safe landing, no beacon, no emergency landing fields, and no aerial maps — and no parachutes. Culver and Edgerton came down safely on the bumpy landing strip. The terminal was well marked beside the Lincoln Highway and the barn-like hangar was unmistakable. They knew they had reached the right place although Paul said the fog was so thick that as he approached Philadelphia suddenly there loomed before him, out of the mist, the statue of William Penn on top of city hall. "I could have reached out and shaken hands with him, as I flew by" Paul told us. This at least told him where he was! His magnetic compass was some help, but it wasn't accurate. The pioneer flyer had no reliable compass he could count on. He could follow railroad tracks, and he could dip down to read the name on the depot when the visibility was good enough but he had to have a natural instinct for cross country flying. He simply had to fly by the seat of his pants!

The crew on duty at Bustleton dashed out to greet Culver and Edgerton, looked over their newly converted Curtiss Jennies, and rolled them into the hangar for further inspection. These airplanes looked different, with the mailhatch in place of the front seat. Then a red, white and blue stripe had been painted on the tail and a star on the underside of the lower wing as an aerial-mail distinguishing mark. The varnished linen of the fuselage glistened with newness, as did the shiny wooden struts, and wooden propeller and the taut wires which braced the wings of the biplane. There was the fresh odor of banana oil, an ingredient of the dope with which the linen surfaces were painted. The crew realized these airplanes were special and they gave them all the attention a race horse receives on the day before a race.

One is reminded of the similarity of the air mail service to the Pony Express of the earlier, slower, more primitive method of carrying the mail, when one rider would relieve another as his bags of mail were transferred to a fresh mount and he would speed off to this next relay point. It was important then to keep the ponies in good shape for this duty, and so it was with the more modern carriers of Uncle Sam's mail, who were relying not on pony power but upon a more modern version — horsepower. It took courage and stamina to blaze the forested trails through the wilderness, and it took the same qualities to blaze the sky trail.

There was plenty for Culver and Edgerton to do as they waited for Major Fleet to arrive. They inspected their planes and made minor adjustments. There were so many things wrong with those early airplanes and with their motors that the crew who had worked all night on them still were not satisfied. But they knew Major Fleet would give the final inspection when he arrived.

They stepped outside to scan the sky for the tiny speck that would mean he was on his way. He had taken off at the same time they had, but with a limited supply of gas, perhaps 19 gallons. They knew an old timer like Fleet would make if all right, no matter what. For even his name augured well! As he was to relate it to Paul some years afterwards, he had climbed up through the fog and come out at about 11,000 feet, almost the ceiling of his airplane, and had flown by magnetic compass and the sun until he ran out of gas and the propeller had stopped. He glided down in the direction of Philadelphia, selected a likely farmer's field, and landed his plane intact.

He climbed out of the cockpit and approached a startled farmer, asking if he had any gasoline on the place. He had and was glad to oblige. Together they managed to pour gas from a five gallon milk can into the gas tank without a funnel, or chamois to strain it. In those days, gasoline was not refined so it had to be strained through a chamois placed over a funnel. They managed to get about three gallons into the machine, enough so Major Fleet could take off and make Bustleton before dark. But it was no small task to get the motor started without a trained mechanic to spin the prop. The prop had to be pulled over with the whole weight of his body, then he must artfully duck out of the way.

Many a broken arm and even more serious accidents often resulted. The JN6H Fleet was flying carried a booster starter which he had to manipulate by himself. He had to crank the wooden propeller by pulling it through to get compression, run around the wing, jump into the cockpit and accelerate the booster before losing compression.

It took a dozen run arounds before the engine caught. Then about two miles from his destination the engine again coughed, sputtered and died. He was out of gas again with no place to land but a plowed field near the highway. As he climbed out of the cockpit he was greeted by a friendly voice "hello there, can I help you?" It was Charles Sales, one of the neighboring farmers who saw the airplane in trouble and drove along in his Flivver, stopped and ran over to where the plane had landed. The air mail project in their midst was not too popular with the local farmers and villagers but here was one who was interested in all the preparation for the air mail and who often drove over to the Field to see how things were progressing. He was familiar with the personnel there and had even offered food and lodging at his comfortable farm home until adequate housing could be provided for them. It was providential that he should happen along at that moment, rather than some of the other natives. He offered to drive Major Fleet the rest of the way in his car and to help in any way he could.

It wasn't always that easy to get help from a good Samaritan in those days because the appearance of a stranger, especially one dropping out of the sky, dressed in the unfamiliar aviator garb of leather coat, breeches, puttees, helmet and goggles, suggested a visitor from outer space or even worse — a disguised German spy. Once in just such an emergency as this Paul had made his way to the road after running out of gas and making an unscheduled landing, just as a farmer drove by in his buggy. Paul was about to hop aboard for a lift to town when the farmer whipped up his horse into a gallop and was off in a cloud of dust calling back over his shoulder "No siree, I ain't takin' up with strangers."

Meanwhile, as the Bustleton crew came out of the hangar late that afternoon for another expectant look at the sky, they were astonished to see Major Fleet drive up in an open touring car, with Mr. Sales at the wheel. "What happened?" a chorus of voices blurted out. Naturally, they were relieved to see him on the ground at least and unhurt. He hurriedly explained what had happened and gave orders for Culver to take a can of gas — and be sure to take a funnel and chamois — and get into Mr. Sales car and he would drive him to where the plane was down and he was to fly it in at once. Major Fleet and Jim quickly rounded up the few autos at the field and those they could scrape up from farmers in the neighborhood and directed the drivers to stay around and arrange their cars in a row and turn on the car lights so Culver could see to land in the dark if necessary.

At the signal they all lined up and waited in their cars, with lights on as ordered, straining their ears for the sound of a motor in the sky. After what seemed a reasonble period of time and with no word from Culver, they concluded he had decided to wait until daylight. So they turned off their lights and went home.

But Paul had orders to bring that plane in that night and he'd do it! As Paul told afterwards "as I flew toward the Bustleton Field all was darkness! I remembered that I had noticed, as I looked the area over that afternoon for such hazards as telephone wires, etc., and had made a mental note of the row of gas lights bordering Lincoln Highway along which our field was located, so when I arrived over the field and no hangar or auto lights were visible, I still felt I could gauge the field from these highway lights and land safely. I had had practice in landing at night by the light of a row of lighted hangars at Ellington Field in Texas so this should be easy I thought. However, I was not aware that all the roads and highways in Philadelphia county were also lighted by gas lamps and I made the mistake of coming down into a field adjacent to ours which had been newly plowed. As I touched down I realized my mistake and in opening the throttle in an attempt to hold the tail down, the wooden prop struck the ground and shattered. Was there a spare propeller in the hangar? Although I knew there were some spare parts there, they were scarce but I hadn't taken complete inventory that afternoon. My one thought was the aerial mail deadline tomorrow. I scrambled out and made my way up the road in the pitch darkness toward a light in the distance which proved to be a farmhouse. The farmer was in his driveway just ready to leave for the Philadelphia market with a load of chickens. He was startled when I appeared out of the darkness, but seeing my plight he generously offered to take me along in his truck and drop me off at the Field.

"No one was there. The hangar and office were locked so I was unable to get in to check and ease my mind about a spare propeller — and I knew I would have to wait until daylight to get the grounded airplane back to the field. So I walked up the road to the Sales farm where I was told I would be temporarily quartered. No one was there either except the housekeeper who showed me to my room. After setting my alarm clock for daybreak, I fell into a sound sleep. But I didn't need the alarm! Sometime after midnight I was awakened by Major Fleet and Mr. Sales bursting into my room. They had been out most of the night in search of the airplane and me. You can imagine their relief to find me safe and sound in bed because they had heard over in the village, that an airplane had circled overhead in the darkness, and then the motor had cut out and quit — and that was the last that had been heard of it. So, of course everyone assumed that I was down somewhere in the wrecked airplane, injured or even dead. The State Police had been alerted and the search was on. Thanking our lucky stars, we all went to bed and I was up at the crack of dawn next morning and over at the hangar where I found the priceless extra propeller. One of the mechanics drove me over to the downed airplane, put on the new prop, cranked it for me, and I flew the airplane back to the Bustleton Field." Luckily, I knew nothing about all this at the time since I was still in New York at Belmont Park, but when I reached Bustleton I heard many hair-raising tales of what happened on that fateful night of May 14th.

May 15th was the day of destiny. The day dawned bright and clear and when Major Fleet and Jim Edgerton arrived at the field they were relieved to find that Paul had the airplane serviced and ready for use. After checking to see that everything was in readiness and that Jim and Paul understood their orders, it was time for Major Fleet to ferry a mail plane to Boyle in Washington. He chose No. 38262. Paul hoped that he would because that was the one Boyle would fly back to Philadelphia for Paul to proceed to New York with. It was the one he had flown down from the Curtiss factory on Long Island and he wanted to make the return trip in it.

Major Fleet climbed aboard, taxied out to the runway and took off with the crew cheering and waving good luck, leaving Edgerton with No. 38274 and Paul — just waiting. He came down on the Polo Field in Washington's Potomac Park, just a half hour before the aerial mail was to start. It was not an easy field to get into for it was small and surrounded by trees, and worst of all, there was a bandstand at one side. The Park Commissioner had refused to remove any of these hazards, saying that it would take a lot of red tape to get a government order to do so. The pilots would simply have to dodge these encumbrances every time they took off or landed and although the pilots howled their protest it did no good. It seemed such landmarks were more valuable than an airplane or a pilot's life. Eventually Major Fleet took the bull by the horns and without park authority, but certainly as a war-time emergency measure and out of necessity, ordered the mechanics to cut down the most dangerous trees. But the bandstand stayed.

In spite of all that, Major Fleet made a perfect landing on schedule and was greeted by a cheering crowd that pressed against the roped-off area. Lieutenant Boyle was there to greet the Major, all set to go, and glad to see for the first time the plane he was to fly. Major Fleet took time for a quick and private briefing with Boyle. Then he spread a large military road map out on the wing of the plane and pointed out the route north. Then he helped him strap the map to Boyle's thigh with large rubber bands. This was not an aerial map for there were none at that time, but a regular road map. The pilot could glance down at it in his lap as he flew along.

After giving Boyle a few hearty send-off remarks Major Fleet hurried away and it was now up to Boyle who had time to examine the controls in the cockpit, with which he was familiar from his training course on just such an airplane, and he began to count the minutes. The rest was up to the mechanics and crew.

Major Fleet then turned his attention to the formalities of greeting the President of the United States, Woodrow Wilson, who with his beautiful wife had come out from the White House to witness this historic event. They, along with other dignitaries, received a great ovation from the large crowd that pressed against the ropes hoping to catch sight of the "lift off." They had come on foot, with horse and buggy, in wagon, auto and even on horseback. Perhaps the most eager of these spectators, and certainly one who had reason to hold a place in the front row, was six-year-old David Fleet. He knew the air mail would succeed if his dynamic father Reuben Fleet was in charge. Things always did and they always would where his Dad was involved, as was to be proved in the years to follow. He was a little boy who grew up to take his place beside his father in his successful enterprises, notably Consolidated Aircraft. Fabulous good fortune followed Reuben Fleet throughout his long and colorful life.

There was another young man with an aviation future in that crowd whose interest in aeronautics began while watching Orville Wright fly. He, too, was one day to be an aviator, a member of the Early Birds of Aviation and most notable of all the beloved curator of Aeronauts at the Smithsonian Museum — Paul E. Garber.

The President and his wife were a great attraction because in wartime they made few public appearances and people were eager to see them. At that time there was no television to show celebrities to the world daily, so their few public appearances were quite an event. Major Fleet circulated among the guests greeting the President and Mrs. Wilson; Secretary of War Newton D. Baker; Assistant Secretary of the Navy Franklin D. Roosevelt; Navy Secretary Josephus Daniels; Postmaster General A.S. Burleson and his second assistant Postmaster General Otto Praeger who was in charge of transportation of all mail and who worked hard for air mail in our country; and his able assistant Chief Clerk George L. Conner.

Major Fleet chatted with all of them, especially with President Wilson while they waited expectantly for the take off. The President congratulated him on the efficiency and dispatch with which he had hastily organized the air mail project, and in his enthusiasm even suggested that the air mail be extended to Boston the very next day, and that such information be given to the newspapers at once. But Major Fleet persuaded the President to postpone any such extension until the present route should be established and functioning well. Secretary Baker agreed. Captain B.B. Lipsner (not an aviator) had been delegated to take charge that day, to see that all was in readiness.

There was no formal ceremony at the terminal but a dramatic touch was added when a postal truck roared up with four pouches of mail and they were deposited in the hopper. Before closing the lid the postal clerk dramatically drew out a letter and handed it to President Wilson for him to sign his name across the cancelled stamp. This letter addressed to Noah Taussig, 111 Wall Street, New York, N.Y. bore the first 24¢ air mail stamp bought from the Post Office. The distinction of the first air mail stamps was the red, white and blue print which pictured an airplane in full flight. They sold for 24¢ an ounce. This entitled the sender to have his letter forwarded by the Post Office to points beyond, or in case the airplane arrived too late for the regular postal delivery to have it delivered by a special delivery service. The letter to Noah Taussig with its valuable Presidential autograph was later to be presented to the American Red Cross in New York to be sold at auction.

The original four pouches of mail contained more than 6000 letters; 3300 for New York, 300 for Philadelphia and 3000 for redistribution to other addresses throughout the country. The entire weight was 140 pounds (although they could carry up to 300 pounds) and the estimated gross revenue was $1,584.

Many stamp collectors bought first air mail stamps and sent letters with the request that the cancelled stamp be returned to them. One stamp collector alone sent 400 and I will never know why I did not think to send a letter on that first day of air mail, at least to members of my family. I missed a golden opportunity. I should have been as alert to that as I was to saving newspaper clippings about the Air Mail. Those cancelled stamps are worth a fortune today — especially ones with the airplane printed upside down.

And that is a story in itself. A stamp collector named William T. Robey entered a branch post office in Washington on May 14, 1918 to purchase a few air mail stamps. He noticed that the man in front of him had turned back to the clerk a sheet of 100 24¢ air mail stamps because he saw that they were defective and that by an error, the airplane was printed upside down. Mr. Robey noticed that the clerk had tucked the defective sheet under the counter, so after realizing he had a collector's "find" Mr. Robey went back after lunch and persuaded the clerk to sell him the defective sheet and he took it home and hid it for safe keeping. He knew he had something hot that would make philatelic history — for this was the only such sheet released. Mr. Robey later sold the sheet for $15,000 (It has cost him $24.00) By 1960 the value of one single stamp had risen to $6000. Today it is worth a fortune.

Meanwhile, the autographing party was over, zero hour had arrived and it was time to take off. Boyle, somewhat flustered by the bouquet of roses his fiancée handed to him along with a parting kiss, climbed into the cockpit, adjusted his helmet and goggles, fastened his safety belt, glanced down to see if his navigation map was secure, and called out "Contact." One of the mechanics spun the propeller. Nothing happened. Again he pulled it over and still nothing, not even a sputter from the lifeless engine. It was a tense moment for both pilot and crew and by now President Wilson was becoming impatient and indicated he was ready to leave. He had little time to give to extra-curricular activities in wartime, even if air mail was his own brain child.

Suddenly it occurred to one of the crew what was wrong — not a drop of gasoline in the tank! This was an embarrassing moment for Captain Lipsner and Major Fleet never did get over it. He was furious and later wrote: "He failed in his mission and didn't have a drop of gasoline there. We drained gasoline from a British airplane and from two other American airplanes that were on the field and filled the airmail plane."

Then they were ready for a new start and again Boyle called out "Contact" and this time the engine burst into life. The prop began to accelerate into a steady purr and what had been an inert wooden blade suddenly became a bright blur in the sunshine. Boyle gave it the gun and took off with easy grace skimming over the trees and began to climb as the crowd burst into bravos and applause. At last the historic first air mail service was under way, and the Wilsons were glad that they had waited.

President and Mrs. Wilson and the celebrities departed and the others settled down on the grass or in their carriages and cars to await the mail plane coming from the north.

Boyle climbed to the designated ceiling, then made his turn toward Philadelphia, or so he thought, to where Culver was waiting for him. As Captain Lipsner strained his eyes to watch him he was astonished to realize that after circling, Boyle had turned south, not north. Perhaps he was just circling to gain altitude and as the plane disappeared in the distance he hoped that was the case. When Boyle realized his mistake and saw that the terrain below him did not coincide with the map in his lap and that he must be about 25 miles south of Washington he knew he must land before his gas gave out. He cut the switch, glided down, and landed on a plowed field near a highway, nosed over and broke his propeller. Fortunately he was not hurt but his prop was broken and so was his heart I'm sure, for he was as keen to succeed in playing his role in the first air mail as the other three pilots were. He made his way to a telephone, got Captain Lipsner on the wire and told him what had happened. He was ordered to stay with and guard the airplane as well as the United States mail and was told that a truck would come to his rescue as fast as possible. The mail he was carrying was returned to the Capitol by truck and forwarded by the air mail the following day.

Back up at Bustleton all were ready to play their part in this historic event. Because of the publicity, spectators began to gather long before take-off time. Touring cars, trucks, horses and buggies and farm wagons lined up along Lincoln Highway. Curious onlookers who came out from the city and from nearby farms and villages brought their families and picnic baskets. They sauntered over to look at the fragile biplanes and milled about good naturedly greeting friends and acquaintances. The crowd was in a holiday mood. But they pressed too close, some wanting to sign their names on the canvas fuselage and wings, others attempting to climb all over the plane or to slice off a strip of the linen surface as a souvenir. They brought along autograph books for the two aviators to sign and they were glad to oblige, but when it finally became too much of a good thing and the guards seemed unable to restrain the crowd any longer, they hastily roped off the field and hangars until take-off. The wisdom of this was plain, for since we were at war, sabotage even to air mail airplanes was possible. After a few days of this hysteria, all the air mail planes were closely guarded and inspected and the public was not allowed to get near them because it was discovered that someone had tampered with some of the wire supports of one of the planes. They had been sawed through, nearly to the breaking point.

But on this day the crowds shaded their eyes and peered into the sky for the first glimpse of the mail planes coming from both north and south — or listened for the drone of their motors. It was a patient but expectant group and no one watched more eagerly or intently than the two air mail pilots Paul Culver and James Edgerton, who could only wait, much as the Pony Express riders of pioneer days, ready to leap aboard their mounts. Shortly before 11 A.M. a small Post Office truck came tearing up the pike with its sacks of air mail. The guards lowered the ropes momentarily for the trucks to come in and drive alongside the waiting plane. Here the Post Office crew took over. They tucked the two pouches, bound for Washington into the front seat hopper of Edgerton's plane, but did not secure the strap, because the New York mail had to be included when it arrived. "So far, so good" they thought as they again trained their eyes and ears on the sky.

Some post office employees from Philadelphia passed out little red, white and blue cards among the crowd, on which was printed the complete air mail time table, for all three terminal points, and that made it look very official!

Suddenly the phone in the little shed began to ring. It was Lipsner calling for Paul, giving him the bad news and ordering him to fly Webb's plane No. 38278 right back to New York as soon as he landed, taking the Philadelphia mail only.

After the initial shock there was nothing to do but stand and wait. As for Culver, he didn't even try to conceal his feeling over what had happened. He just paced back and forth and tried to be civil and answer questions from the crowd.

Then someone shouted "there he comes" and there was Torrey coming in out of the blue. He made a perfect landing and climbed out. Imagine his surprise to be told about Boyle and that Culver would be using his plane for a return trip to New York! The postal clerks tore open the hopper and tossed the New York mail into Edgerton's plane and the sacks bound for Philadelphia into the waiting truck to be rushed into the city. It was all done with such dispatch that within six minutes Edgerton was off the ground and headed toward Washington. He landed there at 2:50 and was greeted by a great crowd — almost like a conquering hero.

While the mechanics refueled No. 38278 Torrey had time to brief Culver on what to expect up at Belmont Park and on what had happened before his take off that morning. He had come out to the field early to check on Curtiss' biplane No. 38278 which was to be his mount for the day and which he knew like a book — having helped to assemble it. Steve Bonsal had flown over from Mineola to act as his back-up pilot and all was in readiness. They knew there was to be some sort of ceremony to inaugurate this "First Air Mail" because a speakers platform had been erected near the race track, but they were hardly prepared for the extent of the celebration. Schools from nearby communities had been closed so that pupils could see the take off of this historic event. A brass band arrived and then a special train came out from New York City carrying several hundred persons, among them postmaster Thomas G. Patton, Byron Newton, Collector of the Port of New York, Allen Hawley, President of the Aero Club of America, members of the Webb family and many others. This was the most formal celebration of the three terminals that day, and most of the space on the front page of the New York newspapers was given to reporting the event. Such complete coverage had not been given before to an aviation event.

Mr. Patton opened the ceremony with an enthusiastic speech which included these words: "This is a historic moment in the transfer of intelligence. There may be lapses, as there have been lapses in other services, but in its beginning I know I shall receive the encouragement and cooperation of the people of New York, who are never asked to do anything that they do not successfully perform."

Mr. Newton then recalled to his listeners some of his personal experiences as a newspaper correspondent when aviation was in its infancy. He remarked that some of them perhaps had attended the first aviation meet right there at Belmont Park eight years before, and what progress has been made since then. "Ten years ago this morning," he said "I sent to the New York Herald the story of a Wright brothers' flight at Kill Devil Hill. Nobody believed they could fly. Mr. Bennett, editor of the New York Herald, cabled from Paris 'go down and expose this humbug.' Mr. Bennett was usually a good prophet, but singularly had no faith in the Wright brothers. When the Wrights flew over our heads there in the sand hills, we correspondents stood with cameras, and not a shutter clicked — so dumbfounded were we. I telegraphed the story to my paper that the Wrights were really flying. When I returned to New York I found that Mr. Bennett had suspended me for six weeks because I had put over an unpardonable fake."

The aviation industry was represented by several other notables besides Allen Hawley and Henry Woodhouse, Chairman of the Board of the Aero Club of America, all of whom optimistically predicted success for the air mail. Mr. Hawley remarked "this day will go down in history as marking the advent of a new epoch because this New York-Philadelphia-Washington aerial mail line is a forerunner of a network of aerial mail lines which will cover the entire world." He also predicted that within a short time we would see airplanes capable of flying the Atlantic. Another speaker prophesied the establishment of regular passenger airplane routes. Extravagant predictions in 1918!

Another feature of the exercises at Belmont Park was the presentation of Hamilton wrist watches to each of the pilots by Charles F. Miller, President of the Hamilton Watch Company who remarked in his presentation speech that the Hamilton watch had been known for years as the watch of railroad accuracy and it was now destined to become the watch of airplane accuracy. While Major Fleet, Paul, George Boyle and Jim Edgerton were not there to receive theirs, arrangements had been made for their presentation at the respective posts. They are handsome silver watches with the pilot's name engraved on the back. Paul wore his for many years, and I still treasure it. The inscription reads:

Presented to
Lieutenant Howard Paul Culver
A.S.S.R.C.
First Air Mail Service
by
Hamilton Watch Co.

While the ceremonies and speech making were in progress Torrey got the signal to take off. He climbed into the cockpit, adjusted his pith helmet and goggles, gave it the gun and soared off into the sky, reached a height of about 4000 feet and streaked off southward, as the band struck up "The Star Spangled Banner" and the school children sang at the top of their voices. It was a thrilling experience to witness the send off of our first winged postman. Torrey's part in the day's program had gone off as planned and Paul was thrilled to be part of the crowd to greet him as he landed at Bustleton with a pay load of two sacks of mail which contained 182 pieces for Philadelphia; 460 pieces for Washington; three packages and a copy of the previous day's New York Times, weighing in all about 150 pounds.

Now it was Culver's turn and his flight time was past due. It had been a long and anxious wait. He climbed aboard, the mail compartment was closed, the gas tank was full so off he flew with Torrey's blessing. He knew it was now up to him to vindicate the air mail service. The fourth leg must succeed else it would be considered a fiasco and President Wilson's dream would become a nightmare. He opened the throttle, raced down the bumpy field, arose into the blue and disappeared into the northern horizon as the crowd waved and shouted good luck and happy landings. In a little more than an hour's flying time he brought the Curtiss Jenny down for a smooth landing on almost the exact spot where Torrey had taken off. As he neared Belmont Park he was surprised to see several other airplanes in the sky (a rare sight in those days) and they swept over the race track as though escorting a homing pigeon. Some of the pilots over at Mineola had thought it would be a nice aerial welcome, and it did add drama to the event. They flew back to home base as Paul swooped down for a landing at 3:37 P.M. with the Philadelphia pay-load, which consisted of 350 letters; 200 for New York and 150 for points beyond. It wasn't an easy touch down because the excited crowd rushed out onto the race track and Paul barely had space enough to land as the people surged forward. The postal truck, with Harvey L. Hartung in charge, dashed up to the plane, the hatch was unbuckled, the mail pouch tossed into the truck which rushed it, at top speed, to the waiting train. Within minutes the first air mail was on a Long Island special train bound for the New York Post Office, and the opening day was declared a success even though the Washington mail wasn't on board.

Some of the guests who had come out to see Torrey take off that morning returned to the city on the special train, but a few had remained and a large part of the local population was on hand again in the afternoon to watch the second big event — the arrival of Lieutenant Paul Culver with the Philadelphia air mail. As the mail was being removed from the front seat compartment, Paul climbed out of the cockpit, pushed his helmet and goggles back, then tossing his leather jacket aside, good naturedly allowed the crowed to take over. They swarmed around him, shaking his hand, embracing him and pressing their autograph books toward him. The band played, school children again sang "The Star Spangled Banner" as they waved American flags, and everyone was in a festive mood. Then the crowed began to disperse, satisfied that it was the end of a perfect day (almost perfect, that is) and that they had witnessed the start of the world's first regularly scheduled air mail service.

To Paul it was all in a day's work and he was glad to get away from all the fanfare and back to the quiet and luxury of our quarters at the Turf and Field Club. So far, so good, but what about tomorrow? He needed a good night's sleep after all the frustrations and excitement of the day.

Thursday, May 16, the second day of the air mail, was to have its problems too. Edgerton and Boyle were in Washington, Webb and Walter Miller at Bustleton, and Bonsal and Culver in New York. That was the line-up. Boyle was to be given a second chance so he again took off with the Washington mail with Major Fleet flying escort in another plane to accompany him part of the way. When about 40 miles out of Washington, on the correct compass route northward, Major Fleet cut his throttle and called out to ask Boyle if he was O.K. and could carry on alone. He indicated he could and Fleet turned back. But soon Boyle became confused and realizing that he was off his course he landed and found that he was in Cape May, New Jersey. Nothing but lack of gas and the Atlantic Ocean had stopped him. He phoned Bustleton and was told to gas up and come on in. This he did and reached the suburbs of Philadelphia but he could not locate the air mail field at Bustleton so he landed on a polo field near the Philadelphia Country Club. There being no brakes to slow his landing, the airplane ran along the field until it was stopped by a clump of birch trees on the edge of the high banks of the Schuylkill River. A wing was ripped off as the fuselage wedged between two trees. Boyle climbed out, unhurt, and peered over the edge where a hundred feet below was the river. He must have thanked his lucky stars for he certainly led a charmed life. He found a telephone, reported his predicament, and soon a truck loaded with spare parts was on way to his rescue. The mail was sent into Bustleton by truck to be sent on from there.

That was the second strike-out for Boyle. It was plain he had not had sufficient training in cross-country flying so he went back to flying school to complete the training that had been interrupted by his assignment to the air mail service. In the early days of aviation it wasn't practical for a pilot to fly more than a few miles cross-country because of the limited supply of gas he could carry, so most of the flying was done at training centers with the home base always in view and within gliding distance. If the pilot did not have the natural instinct to fly cross-country he was wise not to attempt it. For his own safety Lieutenant Boyle was relieved of the air mail duty, and Lieutenant E.W. Kilgore was selected to replace him.

The air mail pilots were supposed to get the mail through with only short preliminary practice to familiarize themselves with the route, so it was inevitable that during the first few days it did not function perfectly. In fact, it wasn't until the fourth day that all four legs got through without some failure, but after ten days it was running smoothly and from that beginning the air mail was to grow and expand without interruption.

Fate seemed determined to mar their efforts to get the mail through on a perfect schedule. Motor trouble, forced landings, losing the course, and bad weather conditions would have discouraged the less intrepid. To cite a few mishaps: on the second day of the service May 16, a haze over the Delaware River made visibility poor and so upset the schedule. Unable to see the Philadelphia field Lieutenant Bonsal, who was flying the mail down from New York, had to make a forced landing on the Bridgton Race Track, about 35 miles from his destination. Some horses grazing there refused to scatter as the airplane came down, and in dodging them, Bonsal steered into a fence, damaging the plane so much that it had to be taken to Bustleton on an Army truck. Another permanent landing! The New York mail was accordingly sent into Philadelphia in a Post Office truck.

On that same day Lieutenant Edgerton, who flew the Washington mail north to Philadelphia, unexpectedly made the first round trip! Lieutenant Walter Miller, who flew the Philadelphia-Washington relay, had turned back to the field when only about 25 miles south, and because of motor trouble had returned to the Philadelphia field. Edgerton, who had already landed, offered to make the return flight to Washington with Miller's pay-load. That double relay was considered quite a feat for Edgerton. In fact, his entire air mail record was excellent.

On the third day Paul, who was still in New York waiting for his turn at the relay, flew the mail to Philadelphia on schedule and the other pilots carried out their schedules so at last things were moving along as planned, and as time went on there were fewer interruptions. Undaunted by the mishaps of the first few days, the pilots and the officials felt confident that the service would improve as they became more familiar with the work. Soon the Post Office Department realized the need to provide emergency landing fields along the route and suitable fields were selected at Harve de Grace and Baltimore, Maryland; New Brunswick, New Jersey and Wilmington, Delaware. They were rarely used, but to know they were there gave the pilots greater assurance.

After two weeks of supervising the air mail, and feeling confident that the pilots whom he had chosen were ready to carry on without him, Major Fleet returned to his urgent duties in Washington. The air mail pilots continued to justify his confidence in them until their job was done and they could return to Army duty and the civilians took over. Major Fleet was more fortunate than Paul in that he got overseas duty. He sailed for France on the Leviathan on October 7, 1918 along with Colonel "Hap" Arnold, Major August Belmont and others who had done so much for the war effort as well as for the air mail.

The three terminals continued to attract daily crowds but the amount of mail carried decreased decidedly after the first few days. However, the public was gradually convinced of the usefulness of air mail and as the volume increased it was necessary to provide airplanes capable of carrying larger pay loads. The powerful Liberty Motor, which American aviation had been waiting for, was adapted for air mail use as was the DeHavilland (DH-4) airplane and these made for greater speed and efficiency. Daily flights and more reliable schedules were maintained and air mail became a matter of course. It is significant and much to their credit that there were no fatalities nor serious injuries in the three months that the Army pilots flew the mail. The average regularity of flights was better than 80% for the first month and during the last two weeks of that month only one flight was missed, because of an electrical storm.

By the middle of August when it was apparent that the air mail service was well established, the Post Office Department began to recruit civilian aviators to replace the Army flyers and to contract with civilian aeroplane companies to carry the mail in place of Army airplanes. War surplus provided all the pilots, engineers, mechanics and airplanes that were needed. Paul and the other pilots were officially relieved of their duty on August 29, 1918 and the civilians picked up where the Army left off, flying the mail for many years with great success, with the exception of that later disastrous period when President Franklin D. Roosevelt took the air mail subsidies away from private airlines and gave them to the Army because of suspected irregularities and kickbacks. He, no doubt, carried the image of the success of the first air mail when in the beginning, the Army flew it without any fatalities. But this time many Army pilots were killed because they were ill prepared for the assignment, which by then covered longer and more hazardous routes across the nation. The public roared its indignation.

The original air mail service between Washington, Philadelphia and New York grew into a pattern which spread out over the entire continent and subsequently extended around the world. The romance of the mails is a saga of courage, resourcefulness and dedication that went through many testing times and produced many an unsung hero. These men carried out the plans which the Post Office Department began to formulate in the spring of 1918 and helped air mail make aviation history and it fulfilled its original purpose, even to producing the greatest of all air mail flyers Charles A. Lindbergh. No doubt it was while flying the mail between St. Louis and Chicago that the "Lone Eagle" began to dream of flying across the ocean and then made that dream come true in the most dramatic flight of the time, flying alone and non-stop from New York to Paris in 1927.

Nowadays air mail is no longer carried on special airplanes, nor does it even have a special stamp, but on commercial airlines along with other baggage and passengers, and travels at speeds never even imagined in pioneer days. The extravagant predictions made at its inauguration in 1918 have come true and have even been surpassed. The declaration that airplanes would one day be capable of flying across the ocean seemed too fantastic to even consider at that time, but it came true within ten years.

Meanwhile, as air mail lines expanded across the country, more and more pilots were added to the roster and it was natural that their mutual interest should eventually draw them together into an organization called "Air Mail Pioneers," an affiliate of the National Aeronautic Association. It is an organization of, by and for the former employees of the U.S. Mail Service, Post Office Department, between May 15, 1918 and August 31, 1927, whose purpose is to keep alive their memories and mutual interests, and to preserve for posterity the priceless mementos of the years when individual pilots flew the mail.

I am proud of my husband's membership in this organization. His certificate reads:

> "*Certificate of Membership*
> *Air Mail Pioneers*
> *H. Paul Culver*
>
> *having the distinction of being an employee of the Air Mail Service is hereby awarded this certificate of life membership in the Air Mail Pioneers.*
>
> *The Post Office Department established and operated the Air Mail Service in the United States between May 15, 1918 to August 31, 1927. Personnel of the Air Mail Service flew the airplanes and operated the ground facilities required to maintain and support this service. This was the world's first scheduled air line, the forerunner of todays' commercial air transport service.*
>
> *The pioneering achievements of the Air Mail Service were recognized by award of the Collier Trophy in 1922 for completing a year's operation from coast to coast in all weather conditions without a single fatal accident and again in 1923 for having successfully demonstrated to the world the complete practicability of night flying in commercial transportation."*

This group gets together regularly for regional and national meetings. Paul and I were privileged to attend the meeting held in Washington on May 15, 1958 to celebrate the fortieth anniversary of the start of the Air Mail and to be present at the unveiling of a marker in Potomac Park by Colonel James Clark Edgerton on the very spot where he had landed with the first Air Mail May 15, 1918. We regretted that the Fleets and Webbs were not there but they planned to come on from their California homes to attend the Golden Anniversary in Washington May 15,1968; and the Edgertons to come on from Florida. But Paul Culver was not to be there because he made his last flight into The Great Beyond on June 24, 1964. His wife and children were there to do honor to his memory.

Present at the 1958 ceremony were several Post Office employees who had been there on that historic day and the guest of honor was Mrs. Woodrow Wilson, who though near the end of her life, seemed to relish a visit with Jim and Paul as she recalled that May day in 1918 when she and her husband had been on hand to watch it all start.

This reunion brought back memories of the time when the Army pilots were relieved of the air mail project the end of August 1918 and went back to regular duty. We could have paraphrased the familiar college song "Where, oh where are the Air Mail pilots? Safe now in the wide, wide world."

Before they left the Air Mail Service the Army pilots received letters of commendation for their work. Paul's read:

Dept. of Military Aeronautics
Washington D.C.
July 25.18.

From: Officer in charge U.S. Aerial Mail Service. Washington D.C.
To: Lieut. P. Culver. A.S.O.R.C..Philadelphia Station. Pa.
Subject: Record of efficient performance.
1. In view of the transfer of the first U.S. Aerial Mail Service Washington D.C. to New York City, N.Y., this office extends its appreciation of your service as a pilot, flying mail planes on its route.

The service represented pioneer work in many instances, especially in aerial navigation, and constitutes arduous and hazardous service, in so far as the regularity of mail deliveries frequently necessitated aerial flights in such inclement weather as to jeopardize the safety of the pilot.
2. Your devotion to duty as an officer, and efficient performance as an Aviator, render your services distinctly valuable to the Air Service of our Army.

C.A. Willoughby
Capt. U.S. Infty.
Att. A.S.

6
Armistice

Paul's orders, dated August 29, 1918, stated that he was to report to the Department of Military Aeronautics in Washington, D.C. Upon arrival, he found he was to be attached to Bolling Field near the city. His duties were to consist of experimental flying and aerial map-making which involved flying an aerial photographer up and down the Potomac River while he snapped a succession of pictures which when fitted together made a mosiac map of the area. I wonder what Lieutenant Cassidy, his camera man, would think of current aerial shots, taken from many miles up and which show the entire world.

Not so monotonous was Paul's work when he flew one of the airplanes which carried the apparatus for experimenting with the early wireless telephones sending messages from airplane to airplane as well as to the ground. Colonel Culver (no relation) was in charge of this, and one day one of his officers briefed the pilots before take-off with this admonition: "Watch your language. No profanity up there." It seems President Wilson was so intrigued by this experiment that he had a receiving set installed in his office, and he was often shocked at what came out of it!

That was what Paul was doing when the news of the Armistice flashed across the world on November 11, 1918 (to say nothing of the false Armistice rumor of November 7 which preceded this happy day). It seemed too good to be true. Washington went wild. Thousands of hysterically happy people surged through the streets, cheering, shouting, embracing everyone in sight, and singing for joy. Paul was on duty at Bolling Field when the news broke. He and several other flyers were ordered to stand by as plans were hastily made for several airplanes to take part in the celebration which had already begun. By early afternoon they had made up a flight plan in which a formation of a half dozen Army airplanes was ordered to fly over the city, looping the loop in unison, and to frolic about in the sky to express their joy that the war was over. All eyes were upon them as they dipped in salute over the White House. It was a thrilling sight and no one was more excited than I as I stood in the crowd watching, knowing that Paul was flying one of those planes. I must have unconsciously exclaimed "beautiful flying! Nice work Paul" because a woman standing near me looked at me so quizzically that I told her with pride that one of those pilots up there was my husband. "You poor dear," she said patting my shoulder sympathetically. "How can you stand it? Aren't you scared to death?" As other curious eyes turned questioningly toward me I gathered my small son up in my arms, and made my way to the back of the crowd. It seemed a foregone conclusion that if you were the wife of an aviator you would soon be a widow but somehow I thought that the increased use of airplanes during the war had changed that attitude. Apparently not yet.

When the aerial celebration was over Paul and my sister Helen Dodd joined us at the New Willard Hotel (the scene of our wedding two years before) and together we joined the crowds of merry-makers until the wee hours. It seemed providential that on that thrilling night we should by chance meet two of our closest friends of the early days of aviation: Captain Thomas Baldwin, the famous pioneer aeronaut who was in charge of the Curtiss Flying School where Paul had trained, and Victor Vernon who had been his first instructor. What a happy reunion with those two great gentlemen. We had known Captain Baldwin by the familiar and unofficial term of "Cap," but here he was, a bona fide Army Major in olive drab uniform with silver wings on his breast pocket. He had just returned from wartime duty in England. He greeted us warmly, for we were part of his large flying family and as he did so he proudly tapped the oak leaf on his shoulder saying "you see, I am a real Major now." After an evening of reminiscing about the good old days and about his war experiences, and before bidding us good night, he turned to Vic and Paul and said, "Now boys, let's go back to Newport News and get back to work!"

As fate would have it, we did not go back until 40 years later, only to find the place deserted where the Curtiss Flying School and Atlantic Coast Aeronautical Experimental Station had once flourished and dominated the scene. There was only empty space there on the shore of Hampton Roads where aviation had once made history. There wasn't even a marker for remembrance. Paul and I sat in our car sadly viewing the spot which had known such aviation activity in 1916.

It is all too true that you can't go back and live your life again, but you can relive in some memory experiences which you shared and cherished long ago; and that is exactly what we did as we traced each step of Paul's life-long love affair with aviation which began in 1911 and was to continue to journey's end.

Like most service men Paul asked for his discharge from duty after the Armistice was signed on November 11, 1918, so he could be home for Christmas. Everyone, weary of the war, was eager for discharge papers or at least for a furlough. Joyous reunions were occurring everywhere over the happy holiday. Peace on earth seemed real, at least for the moment.

When the new year began there were decisions to be made whether to return to the air mail service because of the telegrams that kept coming urging him to do so, or to stay at home and go into the family business. We were awaiting the birth of our second child so it seemed best to stay put at least until May when the baby was due. By then Paul was so involved with business and family that he felt duty bound to push his yen for aviation farther out of mind although I am sure he longed for the more thrilling life of aviation. He at least was making a living but many of his flyer friends were having a real struggle. Aviation slumped almost to a stand-still after the war, and there were many war-time pilots and mechanics looking for jobs. Some went into barn storming and a few found other jobs. Some of the family men hung on to the best available places in aviation. In retrospect and with more than 90 years behind me, I wonder if Paul should not have returned to aviation which was his real niche in 1919. As a youth he had all of the qualifications for that more adventurous life; he was audacious, fearless, determined but then he fell in love and love does strange things to people. Beside romance, it brings responsibilities and obligations and in his case "clipped his wings." But he was never far from aviation. He kept in close contact with it and with old friends whom he met at the air races and at Early Bird reunions and by keeping in touch with aviation's amazing progress.

Paul returned to the engineering profession for which he had been trained and he found his real niche as a sales engineer with the Ex-cello-O Corporation of Detroit, Michigan, builders of machinery for the aircraft industry among other things. He retired in 1957 and returned to his native Wisconsin where he lived until his passing in June, 1964.

That is what I was thinking about on that day of August 31, 1983, when Paul's picture was flashed on the television screen during a program on the ABC "Good Morning America" show honoring the Early Birds. It was timed for the day after one of the more important Space Shuttle flights to call attention to the vast difference between the two eras. The Early Birds were represented in a lively dialogue with David Hartman, the host, by Forrest Wysong, the president of the Early Birds and by Paul E. Garber, curator Emeritus of Aviation at the Smithsonian, and it was my great honor to represent the Early Bird wife. That no doubt gave me the impetus to try to merit such a fine title, by my writings, to revise my 1971 book entitled "The Day the Air Mail Began" and to incorporate it in this book.

But back to previous times.

7
In the Beginning

Our real introduction to the airplane was way back in September 1911 when Beckwith Havens arrived at our home town of Ashland, Wisconsin to do exhibition flying in his Curtiss pusher at our County Fair. Well I remember how excited the crowd was to be introduced to this handsome young hero from the East at a recepton held for him at the Elks club. He had all the glamor of the current movie star, Wallace Reid, clad in tweed knickers and belted sports jacket which were the latest fashion. But young Paul Culver was impressed for an entirely different reason, namely the skill with which Havens took his Curtiss airplane off the ground and flew graceful figure eights above the race track. Paul fell in love with flying and from that day on he vowed that nothing could keep him from being an aviator just like Beckwith Havens.

Many years later at an annual meeting of the Early Birds of Aviation, we were to tell Beckwith Havens that story. He was still as handsome and attractive and he remembered that Ashland date. He recalled how he had taken an open street car from town, up Cemetery Hill to the end of the line, walked through the cemetery which adjoined the Fair Grounds to where his airplane, still in its crates was waiting to be assembled. With the aid of his mechanic it was unpacked and the motor tuned and ready for take-off. Haven's performance was the drawing card of the Fair that fall. No one in this area had ever seen an airplane before. After completing his contract with the Fair committee which called for three hops, one each day, he and his mechanic knocked down the plane, packed it and the engine in their wooden crates for shipment. After seeing them safely aboard the freight train, aviator and mechanic took the passenger train to the next booking. That was how it was done, a slow but sure way to get an airplane from place to place in the early days.

About that same time another pioneer aviator came to nearby Ironwood, Michigan, to do exhibition flying and Paul was on hand there too to watch him uncrate the airplane parts and assemble what looked like a "jig-saw puzzle with motor." But the aviator, Jimmy Ward, put it together, warmed up the motor and took off. Paul marveled at the skill with which he handled his frail flying machine. Jimmy was one of the most popular of the early exhibition flyers. We were to know him at Dayton, Ohio in 1917, but later to lose sight of him until one day Paul was solicited for funds to give Jimmy a worthy burial. It seemed that somehow, after his death in Florida, he had been buried there in a pauper's grave because there was no one to take charge. When his flyer friends learned of it they took up a collection to correct the sad mistake. They were determined that this indignity should not happen to one of the greatest of pioneer flyers.

Meanwhile Paul's determination to learn to fly had taken firm root, and it grew during his Prep school days and on into his college years. After he attended the great air meet in Chicago in 1914, he found it impossible to keep his mind on the mechanical engineering course which he was taking at Lewis Institute (presently known as Illinois Institute of Technology) and he began to slant his courses toward aeronautics, to write letters to the few aviation centers which were well known at the time inquiring about the possibility of attending a flying school, and to make plans to get into aviation. He wanted the best flying school available. His old friend Walter E. Lees, whose career he had followed with great interest, was a flying instructor at the Curtiss Aviation School at Newport News, Virginia at the time, so Paul began to correspond with him early in 1916, asking for advice. Watler mailed him a catalogue and followed that with an application blank for him to fill out for flying lessons on the Curtiss flying boat which was Walter's chief interest. The catalogue made it sound so easy. It said "any man who had driven a fast automobile or motor boat can handle a flying boat in the air after a few lessons. It requires less skill, in fair weather, than any other type of motor driven vehicle, for one has all the world of space in which to maneuver. There are no trees, rocks, or sharp corners, passing vehicles or pedestrians to watch; one's speed is hardly noticed, and it is simply wonderful exhilaration, a feeling so unique that it is difficult to describe." Excited by such glowing propaganda, Paul returned his application blanks. He was accepted. The next thing was to try to persuade his reluctant parents to finance him. They finally agreed and Paul was on his way to a career in pioneer aviation, and to transfer his entire interest from Chicago's westside to this very different kind of school on the shore of Hampton Roads, Virginia, just outside of Newport News at a point known as the little Boat Harbor.

Right: *Maj. Gen Foulois: Orville Wright's companion. At Princeton Flying School.*

Below: *Paul Culver in training airplane.*

Left: *Princeton students take lessons in the hazardous art of flying. June 6, 1917.*

Right: *Schedule of air fares. Sign on the Club House at the Curtiss Aviation School. Newport News, Virginia, 1916.*

Below: *Captain Thomas S. Baldwin in his "Red Devil" in 1912. Glenn Curtiss in the background.*

ATLANTIC COAST AERO·NAUTICAL STATION

·**SCHEDULE OF AERIAL FARES**·

	AND RETURN		ONE WAY
NORFOLK	$35.00		'20.00
JAMESTOWN	' ' '50.00	' '	'40.00
RICHMOND	' ' '200.00	' '	'150.00
WASHINGTON	' ' '500.00	' '	'375.00
BALTIMORE	' ' '500.00	' '	'375.00
PHILADELPHIA	' ' '750.00	' '	'600.00
ATLANTIC CITY	' ' '800.00	' '	'600.00
ASBURY PARK	' ' '1000.00	' '	'750.00
NEW YORK	' ' '1250.00	' '	'1000.00

ALTITUDE FLIGHTS & SPECIAL TRIPS TO ALL POINTS.

Left: *The Duck, 1917.*

Curtiss Aviation School, Newport News, Virginia.

First five members of the Officers Reserve Corps of the Army Signal Corps: (l to r) H. Paul Culver, William Schauffler, Bill Rolfe, Harold Gallop, Walter Barnaby.

At Hammondsport, N.Y. in 1910, bloomer-clad Blanche Stuart Scott was the first woman to fly slolo. With her instructor Glenn Curtiss.

Edith Dodd Culver and Katherine Stinson at Richmond Fair Grounds, October 1916.

Above: *President Wilson with Major Fleet.*
Left: *The upside-down stamp.*

Torrey H. Webb who flew the first Air Mail from New York to Philadelphia,
May 15, 1918.

Lieut. Culver delivering the first Philadelphia air mail in New York.
Below: *Facsimile of special postmark for first air mail letters.*

Air Mail plane and postal truck which received the mail.

The Curtiss "Autoplane" of the 1917 air show.

Returning hero Walter Lees and family.

Paul Culver's Early Bird certificate.

Early Bird reunion, Dayton, 1950's.
Paul Culver is at the top.

8
The Curtiss School

The Curtiss School campus — if you could call it that — consisted of an area at the water's edge where stood a small club house, an early version of a student center, and which also housed the manager's office. Nearby stood a huge barnlike structure called a hangar. There were a few sheds scattered about which contained motor blocks for testing engines, the drone of which went on endlessly. There was a dope shop, which emitted the perpetual odor of banana oil, an ingredient of the dope used to varnish the linen fuselage and wings, as already mentioned. There was no stockpile of spare parts in the shop. When a part was broken the airplane had to be grounded until a new one could be made. The repair shop also contained a few wooden struts, one or two extra wooden propellers, a few bolts of linen, and an old foot-powered sewing machine to stitch it up on; some extra wire and and a few fittings and the mythical "sky hook" which was part of the initiation at the Curtiss School. Rookie flyers often looked everywhere for the "Sky Hook" which they said their instructor had ordered them to take with them on their first flight. More than one fledgling bit on that one!

At the water's edge there was a wooden landing ramp over which the flying boats and seaplanes were launched, and there was a flying field nearby which was actually only a strip cut through a farmer's hay field. That was the complete picture of the school, unless you included the little restaurant across the road, called the Greasy Spoon, where the flyers gathered for a cup of coffee and a sandwich.

This particular Curtiss flying school, owned and operated by the Curtiss Company under the capable supervision and management of the famous pioneer aeronaut Captain Thomas S. Baldwin, was also known as the Atlantic Coast Aeronautical Experimental Station. That accounted for the conglomeration of monstrosities which were housed in the big hangar, some placed about on the floor and others hanging from the ceiling, which answered my query, "why call that big barn a hangar?" It was a completely new word for me. No door of that period would have been large enough so the entire front of the hangar was covered by a huge canvas curtain, which, when open, revealed the most unbelievable collection of early experimental airplanes. Some of these planes had three wings, some two. Some were monoplanes, some triplanes, some were amphibious, and some shaped like actual birds. "The Duck" was our name for the largest of these. I was to watch this "duck" in actual flight and to photograph it off the ground one day when Victor Carlstrom, the famous Curtiss test pilot, flew it in an experimental flight. There were some early Curtiss pushers there too. One day Early Bird Walter Bullock gave us a thrill by flying one of these which he had purchased. He didn't look too secure seated on the frail framework with a motor suspended behind him.

Then there was a plane called the Flying Submarine. This, along with many of the strange airplanes housed there, had been shipped to the Aeronautical Experimental Station for re-assembling for test-flying to prove certain legal claims involved in one of Glenn Curtiss' patent suits at the time. Perhaps the most valuable, historically, was this airplane in which Glenn Curtiss had made his historic flight down the Hudson River in 1910. Actually it was a regular Curtiss biplane mounted on an Old Town canoe, and it was the first aeroplane to take off and land on water.

A large photograph of the historic 1910 flight hung on the Club House wall where it was the object of great curiosity and interest to everyone. Then one day in 1916 Glenn Curtiss himself arrived at Newport News to again fly this famous airplane as all the Curtiss students stood on the shore and watched. Test pilot Victor Carlstrom was to fly it. It was rolled out of the hangar, down the ramp, and into the water. Vic took his place at the controls, two mechanics waded out into the water and grasped the wing tips which were supported by a ski-shaped pontoon arrangement. The idea was that each man was to hang onto these to steady the plane until the momentum of the engine pulled the plane from his grasp. If the plane was held level, it would be able to skim along the water until it gained enough flying speed to take off. Vic Carlstrom tried it several times but was unable to keep it steady. Then Mr. Curtiss took the controls and he showed how it was done. The plane seemed to know its master.

Some time later, the "Duck" was readied for a test hop, also to establish some Curtiss patent claim, we were told. I snapped a picture of it as it was rolled out of the hangar looking for all the world like the King Kong of the bird family. Vic Carlstrom was at the controls inside the glassed-in window in its breast. With the aid of students and mechanics, the "Duck" was wheeled up the hill to the flying field. Vic taxied it to the end of the field so as to take off into the wind, and as all stood around doubtful but hoping, he opened the throttle, and the ungainly "Duck" actually took off and flew a short distance, about half a mile. That was all they asked — just to prove it could get off the ground, and sustain flight for a short period. That point won, the "Duck" was taxied back to its comfortable berth in the hangar, to be dismantled and forgotten.

Victor Vernon was the chief instructor on the Curtiss F boat so Paul was assigned to his class upon arrival at the school. He considered himself fortunate to have his first instruction from the capable hands of this veteran pilot and Vic said he realized from the first that Paul was going to be a good aviator.

The student usually learned to fly the F boat first because the catalogue suggested it and after mastering that, he could go on to fly a land plane. It was said the F boat was easier to fly, and safer, but it never seemed so to me. Perhaps I thought so because I hadn't heard of any fatality up to that time on an F boat. But I had heard of a fatality on a land machine which occurred just before I arrived at Newport News, when Steve Mac Gordon, a famous pilot and a great favorite at the Curtiss School, had died of wounds and burns suffered when his airplane crashed. The atmosphere of tragedy still hung over the school.

There were only about a half dozen young men taking training then with about the same number of planes (Curtiss JN-6's) to fly. Instruction cost one dollar a minute, with only a few minutes of instruction each day. It cost Paul the usual $400.00 to learn to fly and to get his pilot's license from the Aero Club of America and a diploma from the Curtiss School. Captain Baldwin then put him on the pay roll and allowed him to put in extra flying hours to qualify as an instructor on the F boat.

Thus established and being on Captain Baldwin's pay roll, Paul could make plans for our wedding, and for me to join him at Newport News. Everyone without exception thought Paul was crazy to go into aviation and with the approval of his fiancée at that. His parents agreed with this too, especially after visiting at the Curtiss School. One look around was enough to convince them that their son had chosen the wrong profession and they offered every inducement to persuade Paul to give up this dangerous flying business and go back home with them.

While Paul was down in Virginia learning to fly, I was busy writing my graduation thesis for my history major at the University of Wisconsin, struggling with the dry topic "Isthmian Routes to the Pacific Ocean Before 1869." Little did I then know that one day I would know the man who flew across the Isthmus in April, 1913 — Early Bird Robert G. Fowler. He and a photographer named R.A. Dunham made it non-stop in 55 minutes. Quite a contrast to the dreary months and years it took to open up the jungle by the earthbound explorers I was then chronicling!

Paul's letters didn't help keep my mind on my work. Especially when he told of meeting famous names in aviation such as Captain Baldwin, Glenn Curtiss, Major William Mitchell, Captain Tom Milling, Vernon Castle, and so on.

He wrote of Vernon Castle's graduation from the flying school, saying he was as clever and skillful at flying as he was at dancing. I told this to my classmates with whom I had attended a Castle performance in Madison the year before when Irene and Vernon Castle had captivated us by their graceful modern dancing. The Castles were the dance sensation of the day with their Tango and "Castle Walk." They were the exponents of all that was ultra modern, and their modern dancing and dress were already affecting definite social changes. "Why, Irene Castle had the audacity to even bob her hair, which for countless ages had been woman's crowning glory, and I suppose you'd even do that!!," said my friends who warned me that I'd better not let my modern trend carry me that far!

My Gamma Phi Beta sorority sisters were concerned about all this when they gathered in my room and listened to my plans to marry an aviator. They couldn't believe that I would go through with it and subject myself to early widowhood. "Remember, Edith, black is not your most becoming color," they would remind me. They would even repeat half in jest all the gory details of an airplane crash in which the pioneer aviatrix, Blanche Stuart Scott had nearly been killed right there in Madison in 1913. "Don't you know how dangerous it is to fly?" they would add. They could not have foretold nor could I that I would in the distant future know Blanche Scott, and that she would visit Paul and me in our home where we would hear the story of this mishap first hand. Blanche was the first woman to receive a pilot's license in this country and it was Glenn Curtiss who taught her at Hammondsport N.Y. in 1910. In fact she was the only woman he ever taught to fly. She told us that "G.H. said one was enough." But I doubt that he really meant that because he thought enough of her skill to send her out with his exhibition teams along with Lincoln Beachey, Beckwith Havens and others. She was even a member of Captain Baldwin's air circus for awhile. Publicity agents at that time called her "Blanche Scott, the Tomboy of the Air" and "the greatest aviatrix in the world." When the exhibition lost its glamour and became less lucrative, Blanche retired, all in one piece, although she claimed that nearly every bone in her body had been broken at one time or another. Following her aviation career she took to the airways in a new and different way. She became a radio commentator in Rochester, New York with equal success. Her vibrant voice, her poise and zest for living made her a natural in this field. She was an amazing woman.

I had been reared in the north Wisconsin lumbering city of Ashland, in the conservative traditions that prevailed around the turn of the century. Being the daughter of one of Ashland's most beloved physicians and benefactors, my parents took it for granted that after college I would marry the son of one of the town's solid citizens and settle down there. So in 1916, when I announced that I was going to marry an aviator, I might just as well have said that I was joining a circus and marrying the man on the flying trapeze. Up to that time the townspeople had seen only one airplane, and aviation was considered simply as a daredevil stunt. My parents made one stipulation in regard to my marriage: I must finish college, get my degree and teacher's certificate so I would be in a position to support myself when the inevitable happened.

When I fulfilled this parental requirement, and Paul had finished his flying lessons, he telegraphed me that he had arranged for a few days vacation and for me to come on. In spite of all the dire predictions, we were married at the New Willard Hotel in Washington on August 26, 1916 with members of both Culver and Dodd family in attendance. The informal ceremony was followed by a wedding breakfast with my mother as hostess. When looking over the menu, as she planned her party, she was delighted to find an "aviator cocktail" listed. "How appropriate" she exclaimed. But imagine her embarrassment when it was served and it proved to be an alcoholic beverage and not the fruitcup cocktail that was a prelude to luncheons back home. My "teetotaler" mother never did live this down nor did we let her. She often laughed about it afterwards. Paul assured her it was rightly named because it was so potent that it suggested "one drop kills!"

After a short honeymoon we arrived at the Curtiss School where we were greeted with a shower of rice along with hearty good wishes of Paul's friends. Paul was anxious to present his bride to Captain Baldwin and I looked forward to that meeting with genuine anticipation after all Paul had told me about that great man. Imagine my surprise when instead of taking my proffered hand, he took both my hands in his firm grasp, turned searching blue eyes on me and said sternly "so you are the one who is going to ground one of my best flyers!" I knew I needed a appropriate comeback which would prove I already knew quite a bit about aviation and had an unwavering interest in Paul's career. In fact, I was aviation's most ardent fan and I wanted to have a flight as soon as possible myself. So as we chatted, I reminded him that because neither of the Wright brothers had been married, that was no reasonable argument that aviators should not marry. I told him I had read that Orville Wright had remarked that he couldn't support both a wife and his flying. And that Charles E. Taylor, the Wright's mechanic said, when people asked him why the Wrights didn't marry, "Orv used to say it was up to Will to marry first because he was the older, but Will kept saying he didn't have time for a wife." Captain Baldwin seemed amused at my knowledge of the marital status of the various pioneers. He seemed convinced of my sincerity and gave my hand an understanding squeeze. From then on we were the best of friends.

Later, as though to call my bluff, Captain Baldwin arranged for me to have my first flight on September 15, 1916 and it was a tremendous thrill. I must confess that I did feel some qualms when I was asked, before climbing into the F-boat, to sign my life away as it were — that is, to sign a paper absolving the Atlantic Coast Aeronautical Station of any claim in case the F-boat crashed. But I learned this was only routine practice for all passengers.

Paul helped me into the seat at Mr. Vernon's right and the next minute the boat was wheeled around and taxied out across the water. Then, headed into the wind, "Vic" opened the throttle and we cut through the waves like a speed boat, the salt water spraying my goggles, leather jacket, and helmet. Before I knew it we were off the water and in the air. As we circled the hangar I could see Paul and Captain Baldwin shading their eyes with their hands as they peered up at us, and I instinctively wanted to salute them as if to say like Peter Pan, "Look, I'm flying!" I tried to lean nonchalantly over the side of the open cockpit to wave, but the force of the air almost snapped my arm from its socket. We were flying at top speed — all of 60 miles an hour!

We flew out over the Atlantic Fleet which was anchored in Hampton Roads. Sailors rushed out on deck and waved madly and I wished I could wave back but I knew better than to try it again! I realized that we were flying over the very spot where not so long ago the first take-off and landing on the deck of a ship had been accomplished by Eugene B. Ely in a Curtiss pusher. And if my memory of history served me correctly, over the very spot where the battle of the Monitor and Merrimac had given impetus to the Civil War.

After about 15 minutes our flight was over and Mr. Vernon set the boat down on the water so skillfully that I scarcely realized when it hit. It had been a real thrill, and right then I realized that after one had experienced the sensation of flying through the air with the freedom of the birds, he could never again be completely earthbound.

Day after day, as I would wait for Paul to finish his flight, sitting on the comfortable club house porch which overlooked the water on one side and the flying field on the other side, I absorbed, along with the gentle Virginia sunshine, tales of flyers and their adventures that held me spellbound. Why had these lads come here to learn to fly? I guess it was the same old urge that has always lured youth to explore the unknown, to conquer new frontiers, and to meet the challenge of whatever is new and different and untried. That old rallying cry of Horace Greeley's "Go west, young man, go west" had now become "Go aloft, young man, go aloft!" Some thought it seemed futile to stay in college at that time when war clouds were hanging over us. They wanted to join the Lafayette Escadrille and Royal Flying Corps and go to France to fly for the Allies like some Americans such as Eddie Rickenbacker were already doing.

One student was learning to fly for therapeutic reasons, no less. He hoped it would restore his hearing. Another was a grief stricken widower who wished to bury his grief in a new interest. But most of the students were just eager young men looking for adventure.

There were two or three wives there, who would sometimes join these hash sessions at the club house. Some were lukewarm about aviation and seldom came near the school, but Loa Lees and I were almost daily visitors at the Curtiss School where we enjoyed the coed atmosphere which was so much like our recent college life.

An old upright piano in the club house was the focal point around which a group of us got together to sing, and I was glad I could do my part by playing all the popular songs. The students would harmonize the numbers which were the Hit Parade of 1916, most of which reflected the theme of the war being waged in Europe, such as "It's a long way to Tipperary" and "Keep the Home Fires Burning," that nostalgic song written by Ivor Novello, the late British author, actor, playwright and wartime aviator, which was so popular that British troops marched off to France singing it.

Many famous personages in the aviation and political spotlight came to visit the Curtiss School that fall, but to us, there was no greater celebrity than our own Captain Baldwin. He was never away from his post of duty. He would stroll from shop to hangar to flying field, and the rare moments that we could persuade him to sit down and chat a bit were rich in tales of other days. We questioned him often, but he was either too busy or too reticent to tell us all we wished to know about his flying career. But one day Captain George L. Bumbaugh of Indianapolis, a pioneer balloonist and old friend of Captain Baldwin, arrived at the school for quite a long visit and he would talk. Best of all, he brought his voluminous scrapbook with him. And he generously allowed us to pore over it by the hour, answering questions and embellishing the incidents recorded in it. It was a gold mine of information which led me to want to know more about him, too. He and "Cap" Baldwin had been together both in America and in Europe in the early days when balloon racing was all the rage. He also told us what we already knew: Captain Baldwin had done more to advance American aviation than any other person.

9
Captain Baldwin

Captain Thomas Scott Baldwin was born in Missouri on June 30, 1855, the son of a physician. His childhood was spent in Quincy, Illinois so he always claimed Quincy as his home town although he lived in many places around the world. He was called upon to be a man early in life after his parents were murdered by Civil War raiders. At the age of 15 this lone and restless youth left Quincy and went out into the world to make his own way, supporting himself as a newspaper boy, lamplighter, railroad brakeman and book canvasser. As part of his physical fitness fetish to which he was to adhere all his life, he practiced acrobatics on the sawdust pile of the local mill and became very proficient. When selling books at Hot Springs, Arkansas, he met a circus performer named Bryant who was at the Springs for his health and he urged Tom to team up with him in a trapeze act assuring him there was big money in it, but Tom turned the offer down because his real ambition was to be a tightrope walker. He practiced that avidly for three months and when ready to try his luck professionally, made his debut walking a tight rope 30 feet off the ground stretched between two buildings. He was scared to death but the applause of the crowd spurred him on and gave him courage to persevere so he began to give similar performances in nearby towns, passing the hat among the onlookers by way of fee. This amateur work led him into professional status when he qualified to join a circus with which he toured for several years.

In 1883, young Tom teamed up with another young wire walker named William Ivy to play circuses, theaters and amusement parks, featuring the "Japanese slide for life" on the tight wire, which thrilled audiences everywhere. Ivy changed his name to Ivy Baldwin and was known by that name the rest of his life. The caliber of his entire life was summed up when he celebrated his 82nd birthday by walking a 300 foot cable across South Creek Canyon near his home in Colorado. That grand old man passed away October 9, 1953 at the age of 87 and his illustrious name was added to the In Memorium list of the Early Birds of aviation.

By 1885, Tom had worked his way west as far as San Francisco where he persuaded city officials to give him permission to stretch a tight rope from the Cliff House out to the Seal Rocks. On this 700 foot long rope, 90 feet above the roaring breakers where a single misstep would have been disastrous, Tom Baldwin proved that his courage matched his steady nerves. He made this perilous walk every Sunday for many weeks and his fame grew. Only Blondin whose spectacular tight rope walk far above Niagara Falls seemed as brave as Tom Baldwin's feat. He admitted that he was scared and that "it was perhaps the most hazardous and thrilling stunt ever attempted by mortal man, because the rope swung from side to side in the high wind and I was often completely enveloped in fog or in the spray from the surf."

Having successfully carried out this bit of show business he was ready to go up higher and to conquer even greater obstacles: parachute jumping from balloons. He found a balloonist in San Francisco who was willing to take him up, and to watch as Tom made a daring leap into space from a thousand feet and descended with the aid of a parachute of his own design and making.

The story goes that one day he and balloonist Professor Von Tassel climbed into the basket of the gas balloon and slowly took off from an amusement park near San Francisco. Tom stood on the edge of the basket shaking out the parachute and carefully arranging the rope lines. When the balloon reached the required one thousand feet, Tom grasped the trapeze bar of the parachute in both hands and jumped clear. The parachute opened and Tom glided gracefully to earth, aiming his landing area by manipulating the ropes. The cheers of the thirty thousand people inside and outside the amusement park were deafening as he landed safely on target. And thus was born the guided parachute. He kept aiming for a higher altitude from which to leap into space, because he was paid at the rate of a dollar a foot!

Tom's first parachute jumps in California were followed by similar performances all over the country. His own home town of Quincy soon invited him to come home and give an exhibition. He was greeted as a conquering hero. Besides the key to the city, he was presented with a gold medal commemorating his first jump in Quincy: a replica of a balloon, done in solid gold, hanging from a bar set with diamonds.

Was he thinking of settling down and leading a safer life when he married a Quincy girl, Caroline Pool? Indeed not. But he needed a companion and they became not only life partners but business partners as well. Tom's brother Sam joined them in a balloon building venture and also in the building of Baldwin Park at Quincy, an amusement center which flourished for many years.

Fabulous offers were coming to Tom from all over the world so he again went on the road, this time to England. There he received official recognition for his parachute work from the president of the Royal Balloon Society of Great Britain in 1888, who wrote: "I am of the opinion that one of the greatest discoveries in the practical application of aeronautical science has been made by Thomas S. Baldwin. His practical application realizes results which previous to the invention of a reliable parachute seem absolutely unattainable." These Baldwin features made the parachute maneuverable, practical and safe.

In the fall of 1889, Captain Tom and Ivy Baldwin again teamed up for a second world tour which included the far east, where, especially in Japan, the Baldwin troupe was extremely popular. After a successful world encircling tour, they returned home with packing cases filled with valuable presents. These were added to Tom's valuable collection of trophies and gifts, along with decorations from Russia, Italy, Portugal and Spain; from Scientific Societies of France; medals from New Zealand, Egypt, Australia, Java, Sumatra, Mexico, Peru, Brazil, and Japan. He was entertained by kings and prominent personages the world over. He was literally the man of the hour.

On one of his trips to England, Queen Victoria and the Prince of Wales (later to be King Edward VII), witnessed one of his parachute jumps. From a height of about 5,000 feet, Captain Baldwin was able by manipulating ropes to return to practically the point of take-off and he landed within a few feet of where the royal pair was standing. So impressed were they, by this daring and expert performance that the

Queen wished to honor him on the spot and made her wish known to her son. He drew from his own finger a gold ring set with a large diamond and presented it to Captain Tom with the compliments of Queen Victoria and himself. Forever after he wore that ring.

When power came to aviation, he was one of the first to adapt it to the dirigibles which were now absorbing his interest. He built the first successful airship called the California Arrow and flew it at the St. Louis Fair in 1904 and it was a sensation. Then when the airplane was perfected he was one of the first to fly it at exhibitions. He adapted a Curtiss pusher for show purposes and called it "The Red Devil" and his flights were so popular that he couldn't fill all his bookings. The public was so enthusiastic over these performances that they did not question when the notices that went out that the great aeronaut Thomas Baldwin would fly his Red Devil on a certain date, that identical notices were appearing in a half dozen other widely scattered towns. Other pilots substituted for Baldwin under his name on those dates, but that seemed all right with the public. "Seems I was appearing in five different places on the same day. Nice work if you can get away with it," he told us with a chuckle.

Thomas Baldwin popularized aeronautics in America and in Europe, paving the way for the power boys who came later. He encouraged everyone who was working in aeronautics to solve the many problems which presented themselves. He is often called the grandfather of aeronauts in America because of his early and life long devotion to it. He took a keen interest in all of the students who came to him for instruction and followed their careers even after they had left the shelter of his wing. "My boys" he called them with pride and affection. But when they displeased him they were "Damn scamps of the earth" (a favorite expression of his). He used to say that Americans make the best aviators because "there is a certain percent of wild west and Indian spirit in an American lad that makes him quick to think, and to use his initiative to do the right thing at the right moment."

To know Captain Baldwin was a privilege and I have rarely met his equal. At any gathering of aviation pioneers his name is repeated again and again with affection and respect. All aviation pioneers know Captain

Baldwin, the great aeronaut and Early Bird who held pilot license No. 1 for both balloons and dirigibles and Aero Club of American aviator's license No. 7.

He gave good advice to young aviators on the question of health and practiced what he preached. He was the picture of health himself, handsome and rugged and very attractive. He exuded good health and preserved it by good habits, both physical and mental activity, by avoiding rich foods, tobacco and alcohol and recommended "Early to bed and early to rise." He practiced all of these theories religiously. His absolute and unvarying self control went hand in hand with a constitution of steel and these qualities remained until his passing in 1923.

It takes the perspective of time to place any great person in his proper niche in history. The name of Thomas S. Baldwin will grow in stature with the passing of years, and he will be universally honored as he already is in Quincy, Illinois, and where the name Baldwin is familiar to all the oldtimers and where the airport is named in his honor, Baldwin Field.

When that airport was dedicated some years ago, Paul and I made a sentimental pilgrimage to Quincy. We drove out to Baldwin Park, part of which was still standing, and called on a member of the Baldwin family who was still living in the imposing residence which Tom had built many yeas ago, and who was kind enough to invite us in when she learned that Paul was one of Tom Baldwin's "boys." She showed us many of the trophies and handsome gifts which had belonged to her illustrious relative and as we browsed through the various rooms we felt the presence of the great man. It brought back many memories, all of them good.

10
Other Pioneers

Beside Captain Baldwin, the personnel of the Curtiss School in 1916 consisted of a staff of flying instructors, test pilots, and aeroplane engineers and mechanics, among them: Walter Lees, Jimmy Johnson, Victor Vernon, the Hequemburg brothers, Stewart Cogswell, Steve Mac Gordon, Andrew Heermance, Victor Carlstrom, Burt "Fish" Hassel, Stanley Vaughn and many others. Percy Kirkham was in charge of maintenance and repair along with Stanley Vaughn, Jim Honor and Bill Day. Numerous mechanics and engineers came down from the Curtiss factory at Hammondsport and Buffalo from time to time.

The careers of Glenn Curtiss and Captain Thomas S. Baldwin were interwoven from the time when "Cap" first adapted Curtiss engines to his airships and began to experiment with them. Their association continued up to their mutual interest in the Atlantic Coast Aeronautical Station. Since Captain Baldwin was in charge there and always on hand, we got to know him better than Glenn Curtiss who only came to the school occasionally. His visits always caused a stir of excitement and speculation over what new plans those two had for the school and what famous person would show up for the next training class.

Favorable weather conditions at Newport News as well as its proximity to Washington was the reason that Major "Billy" Mitchell came for his flying lesson in 1916. His frequent arrivals would always create a sensation because he was a dynamic, dashing, handsome officer in Army uniform. Paul and I promptly struck up a friendship with him because we too were natives of Wisconsin and I had known his brother Johnny Mitchell in my class at the University of Wisconsin. Whenever I am at the Milwaukee airport which is named in honor of its illustrious son, Brigadier General William Mitchell, I silently salute his handsome portrait which hangs in the lobby.

Jimmy Johnson was assigned to teach Major Mitchell to fly and Walter Lees gave him instruction also. They found him a very apt pupil who was ready to solo after only a few hours. I well remember that fall day when Jimmy turned him loose for his solo. As was customary when a student was making his first solo flight, all other pilots would land and taxi their planes to the side of the landing strip for the safety of all concerned and a white handkerchief was tied to the airplane about to solo. Mitchell's take-off was uneventful but when he circled the field and brought his plane into a landing position, he found he had gained more altitude than on previous turns because he was minus the accustomed weight of the instructor. When he approached the previously arranged spot, he came in too fast for the three-point landing and the momentum of the machine bounced him off the ground. He pulled the plane up, making a half loop and landed and nosed over. There hung Billy Mitchell upside down, strapped in his seat by his safety belt. Paul ran over to him, released his belt, and helped him to his feet. No doubt his pride was hurt but he wasn't, so Paul took a snapshot of the plane, turned turtle. Forever after whenever an airplane turned turtle on landing it was called "a Mitchell." Much later, Paul gave a copy of this picture to Brigadier General Mitchell at one of the aircraft shows in Detroit. At the same time Walter Lees, then chief test pilot for the Packard Aircraft Company presented him with the wheel of the airplane in which he had soloed.

Although the years 1915-16 marked the beginning of the decline in popularity of exhibition flying and the fabulous earnings of the pioneers dwindled to a bare subsistance, many dropped out of it. But a few well-known performers were still at it, and women aviators (aviatrix) were the current big attraction.

When the Norfolk papers reported that the drawing card of the State Fair at Richmond would be the daring woman pilot, Katherine Stinson, we decided we wanted to see her. So on a warm day in the fall of 1916, Paul and I boarded an old stern-wheeler steamboat and took a leisurely all-day trip up the James River to Richmond. That night we went out to the State Fair Grounds and across the racetrack from the grandstand we could see an airplane silhouetted against the night sky by the light of a bonfire.

Using Paul's Curtiss credentials and pilot's license, we were allowed to enter the grounds and pick our way across the field through the darkness to where Katherine and her mechanic, Shorty Schroeder were preparing for her flight. Paul introduced us. The fact that Paul was one of Captain Baldwin's boys was all the credentials we needed.

Katherine Stinson was a surprise to me. I suppose I expected her to be mannish. Instead, she was something quite the opposite, small and quiet-mannered. She appeared perfectly calm as she and her mechanic checked over the plane, revved up the motor to be sure it was running properly and making sure that the magnesium flares attached to the edge of the lower wings were secure. She could well feel confidence in her capable mechanic because he was none other than Rudolph "Shorty" Schroeder who was later to become one of American's most well known aviators. Katherine had discovered this tall gangling six-foot-four-inch mechanic in Chicago when she needed someone to keep her airplane in good shape, and she persuaded him to be a part of her team.

Soon a megaphone announced that the great aviatrix, Katherine Stinson, would make a daring night flight above the field, executing the difficult figure eight maneuver. She took her place in the open cockpit, strapped her safety belt, pushed the visor of her checkered cap around, tucked her curls up into it to keep them out of her eyes. Shorty spun the wooden propeller and signalled Katherine away. She opened the throttle, taxied to the end of the race track, and she was in the air. We followed her maneuvers by the lighted flares which drew luminous figure eights against the dark sky as she circled. The crowd watched, spellbound. Ten minutes later she came in for a landing. Cutting her motor was a signal to those tending the bonfires placed at intervals along the edge of the runway to throw a small can of gasoline on their fires so they would flare up simultaneously to give light to guide her in. She made a perfect landing. Afterwards we sat around the campfire and talked about flying until the dying embers reminded us that it was time for Shorty to stake the plane down, swathe the engine in canvas, and retire for the night.

The next day we joined these two at a luncheon given by the governor of Virginia. In the years to come we were to meet both Katherine and Shorty again at Early Bird reunions and recall this pleasant encounter.

From the time we first met Shorty Schroeder at Richmond he had a full and exciting career in aviation. Later with our entrance into World War I he enlisted in the Army Air Corps and was promoted to the rank of Major, was sent to France and flew with Eddie Rickenbacker's 94th Aero Pursuit Squadron. After the war, he became chief test pilot at Mc-Cook field at Dayton, Ohio, where his experimental flights were front page news, especially the one in which he set the world's altitude record of over 38,000 feet on February 27, 1920, using the first supercharged aeronautical engine. He was later awarded the Distinguished Flying Cross for this flight. In that rarified atmosphere, he lost consciousness, his eyelids froze to his eyeballs, and when his oxygen supply failed, his plane plunged helplessly earthward to within a thousand feet of the ground, when he suddenly came to, got his plane under control and miraculously made a safe landing. He told a strange tale about an incident that happened on that flight. He flew through an area more than seven miles above the earth where there was a cloud bank of tiny creatures, each about the size of the point of a pencil. They clung to the wings and crawled into the cockpit, and even squirmed in behind the instrument panel. These creatures which looked like spiders were still alive when he landed so he sent some of them to the zoology department at Yale University. The professors there said yes, there are spiders in the sky. Young spiders floating on silvery webs are caught up by air currents which carry them up and away, even into the stratosphere. Perhaps these were the same creatures described by some early aviators as cloud worms which they sometimes found on the wings and in the cockpit as well as in their hair and ears.

Major Schroeder suffered from the effects of this harrowing flight into the stratosphere for the rest of his life. His eyesight and heart were affected to an extent that his experimental flying was curtailed and he then turned his attention to the development of the safety factor in aviation. His efforts along this line, as well as his reputation as a pilot, brought him to the attention of Henry Ford who planned to place Major Schroeder in charge of an aviation concern he contemplated in 1925. But Shorty suffered a stroke which rendered him unable to continue his work. He was forced to sit on the sidelines from then on.

Some years ago when I moved to Santa Fe, New Mexico, I was to meet Katherine again but under different circumstances. Since she no longer attended aviation affairs I had lost track of her over the years. On arriving in Santa Fe in 1972, I contacted her at once and was to learn that after her full and exciting life as an aviatrix her health had broken down; she had contracted tuberculosis and had come to Sunmount Sanitorium for treatment.

By the time she had completely regained her health she had fallen in love with the southwest and decided to make it her home. She met and married Judge Michael Otero, a member of one of the fine New Mexico historic, pioneer families. They took their place in civic and cultural affairs of the area and built a Spanish type home in the center of the city. Katherine's hobby was restoring the small Spanish houses nearby, and enclosing the area like a little park, which stands today and is called Plaza Chamisal.

As time went on Katherine contracted an illness that defied diagnosis and finally she lapsed into a coma from which she never aroused. When Katherine passed away in July, 1977, she was honored by a host of friends and by The Early Birds and Air Mail Pioneers and by many prominent citizens of Santa Fe. She was buried in the National Cemetery there at an appropriate graveside service during which a Stinson airplane flew overhead in her honor. The pilot was Dave Allyn who at that time maintained a local aviation museum called "Wings of Yesteryear" which featured many obsolete airplanes.

Katherine's trunks full of aviation treasures were left to her family to dispose of, some to be retained by family members and some for the Smithsonian.

11
Talespins

Back in earlier days, Paul's parents were becoming more reconciled to their son's flying, even to the extent of keeping up on aviation news in the press, because one day in February, 1917, a telegram came telling us that they thought we should attend the First Pan American Aeronautical Exposition being held in Grand Central Palace in New York City, in fact, they were making us a present of the trip.

This first aeronautical exposition meant that the world was recognizing the importance of aviation as a substantial industry rather than a mere sport and it meant that the latest things in airplanes were on display. And a trip to New York was an opportunity to lay in a supply of goggles, helmets, leather coats, breeches, puttees, and ear plugs from the various sporting-good shops. The supply at Newport News had been depleted and these accessories were a necessary part of a pilot's equipment.

This first aircraft show attracted a large crowd, some interested in the planes, some reserving opinions of this new fangled industry, and others smiling their disbelief at what they saw. About a dozen airplanes were on display. Near the entrance hung the original Wright plane. Then there were Curtiss and Wright planes, a Pierce sporting airplane, a Burgess flying boat, and several others, and the hit of the show was the aerial limousine or autoplane designed and built by Glenn Curtiss which was so far ahead of its day as to seem fantastic. It looked like an automobile on wheels with its long hood enclosing the engine, and in its enclosed tapestry upholstered cabin a back seat for two; the pilot's or driver's seat in front, and side entrance door. A four bladed wooden propeller was mounted on the back of the cabin. "That's just for show," someone remarked, "airplanes will never be as comfortable and luxurious as autos!"

After a week in New York we returned to Newport News and our house in a lovely old southern mansion, "The Anchorage," owned by our friend, Dr. Pressey. It had outlived its usefulness to a large family which was now scattering to college and marriage, and they had already taken in Walter Lees, his wife and baby Betty, and the two Hequemburg brothers from New York who were also flyers at the Curtiss School at that time.

Several prominent persons came to our parties there. Among them Fred Duesenburg, who came out to discuss using one of his famous motors in a new airplane called "the Lanzius," which Paul had been urged to test fly.

It was in the Pressey's parlor that we gathered to receive election returns in 1916. We went to bed that night thinking Charles Evan Hughes had been elected President. Next morning we were to learn that Woodrow Wilson had been re-elected on a promise to keep us out of the European war. And yet rumors about war being inevitable seemed to be substantiated by the acceleration of the aviation program. We realized that Washington was preparing for whatever should come.

On Sundays, crowds would come out from town or come across on the ferry from Norfolk to watch the flying and inspect the strange planes in the hangar, or to read the sign that hung on the front of the clubhouse which was a schedule of almost unbelievable prices for flights to nearby cities. People read it and turned away with a smile as if to say "how crazy can you be," incredulous that anyone would risk an aeroplane trip even in an extreme emergency and pay such a price to boot.

One day a ship docked at Newport News, bringing wounded soldiers from the European battlefields, some to return to Canada and others enroute to their homes in New Zealand. Several came out to the Curtiss School. They were glad to see all the activity for they said a surge of airplanes and pilots from the United States could turn the tide of war and bring a speedy victory to the Allies. Some wanted to stay and learn to fly before going back overseas. They told us they had had their fill of the trenches and had applied for aviation training. "I'd rather be shot down and finished off all at once than to wait weeks and weeks in the trenches," they said.

These battle-scarred young men told what they knew about aerial warfare overseas, tales of the heroism of such great aces as Rickenbacker, Lufberry, Guynemer, Thaw and many others whose fame was world wide. They described the thrill of seeing dog fights, a term used for individual aerial combat. To the combat aviator flying was a sporting though deadly game and it is well described by a French Air Force Captain who wrote of it at the time: "It's an amazing game of countless thrills, of soul stirring excitement, a game in which courage, daring, resourcefulness, determination, skill and intelligence achieve honor in life, or if the fates decree, glory in death." When Guynemer was killed, his obituary spoke of him as "a pure jewel of valor and sacrifice." He had bagged 54 airplanes in 215 combats and had been wounded twice before being finally shot down.

In that period of individual combat in the air, the one-seated airplanes, swift, light, and fast-climbing were made to do battle with enemy airplanes and to prevent their planes from crossing the Allies' lines and attacking our scouting planes. In the beginning of aerial warfare there were so few planes that a hostile one was seldom encountered and when one of our pilots did chance to meet one, all he could do was to shake his fist at him or discharge his revolvers at him without the slightest chance of hitting his mark. At this stage, bombs were thrown over the side of the open cockpit without scientific aiming and it was just plain luck when the projectile hit the intended target.

The war speeded up the development of aircraft as no other factor could. Airplanes of greater speed and reliability were built and put into use. One day we were to see the speedy French "Spad" the foreign fighter plane shipped to Newport News for exhibition purposes. Carl Batts who had taught Paul to fly the land machine was chosen to fly it and he looped and rolled at a rate we had never seen before. Those swift planes could fly 120 miles an hour and maneuver with lightning speed. They were armed with a machine gun rigidly mounted on the plane and synchronized to fire through the propeller, therefore capable of shooting only in the direction the machine was flying. It took skill to fly and fire at the same time. It was strictly individual, hand to hand combat, or rather, wing to wing aerial combat and a battle of wits and skillful flying in those early days.

As the war escalated and small groups of planes became engaged in reconnaisance and pursuit flying, aviators were trained for group combat flying much as a football team is trained. It then became a matter of team-work or squadron flying and this also meant a new method of training. Besides fighter pilots, they now needed gunners, bombardiers and observers, to give aerial assistance which the ground troops needed when preparing for battle. They also needed to transport staff officers to strategic positions and to carry aerial photographers to search out all the details of the enemies, such as barbed-wire entanglements, block houses, and net-work of trenches. Earlier, this prepartory work had been done by observation balloons, but these became too vulnerable to be practical in the airplane era. The Curtiss School was soon to have to cope with all these changes and gauge its training program accordingly.

By then, the school was growing by leaps and bounds. Vic Carlstrom flew the big 200 h.p. Curtiss biplane called "The New York Times" to Newport News one day, the one he had flown in a race from Chicago to Governors Island, New York in eight and one-half hours. He was going to take his brother Carl who had come on from his ranch in Wyoming to learn to fly, for a hop in it. But something went wrong and he crash-landed in shallow water before our startled eyes. It was a sorry sight to see the big plane sink into the water with the name "New York Times" slowly disappearing under the waves.

Carl was to be Vic's student that winter and so was Carey Epps, a very pleasant young chap with whom we used to chat at the teller's win-dow at the bank at Newport News. He was at the field every Sunday to watch the flying. He soon resigned his bank job to enlist in the army fly-ing corps and considered himself lucky to be assigned to Vic Carlstrom for instruction. But sadly, in his first trip up when flying at about 3000 feet, something happened. The machine gave a terrific shudder and one of the big wings was torn off. The plane somersaulted to earth and crash-ed with the speed of a bullet, crushing pilot and student before the eyes of horrified spectators.

This tragedy, the first under the new military training program, cast a deep gloom over the school. It took weeks before things were back to normal. As if to snap us out of the shock over Carlstrom and Epps' tragic deaths, our daredevil friend Barnaby gave us something else to think about. Out on solo flight to qualify for his expert's license one day, he climbed up several thousand feet and began to loop the loop and stunt his plane, putting it through terrific paces. The first three loops were fine but he failed on the fourth and narrowly escaped a crash. Captain Baldwin burned the air with a few choice remarks as he watched and didn't breathe easily until Barnaby brought the machine safely to earth. Then he announced in no uncertain terms that "there would be no more looping the loop. While Barnaby got out of it by 'fool's luck,' you can never tell when another would try it and break his fool neck and smash the machine! And we are short of planes too!" Barnaby was in the dog house. Earlier, he earned his nickname "The Dare Devil" by riding a motorcycle along the edge of the Panama Canal locks. It seemed ironical that within a year he would die bravely of wounds received when he was shot down in aerial combat in France.

As war clouds gathered, the Curtiss School took on all the earmarks of a military installation and soon it became an army training center for the Officers Reserve Corps of the Aviation Section of the Signal Corps. Military guards and even a machine gun were sent from nearby Fortress Monroe. A detail was kept constantly on watch for evidence of enemy submarines in Hampton Roads, and Sgt. James E. Carter came from Washington to take charge of the military. New equipment and new personnel arrived. Politicians and officials from Washington came down to check on the progress. Franklin K. Lane, Secretary of the Interior under President Wilson came down to visit his son Franklin K. Lane, Jr., one of the new student flyers. Others in his class were: Bill Colgen, who many years later was in charge of March Field in California; Bob Olds, who became the famous Major General Robert Olds, head of the Second Air Force in World War II, whose untimely death closed a brilliant career, and whose son ace-pilot Colonel Robin Olds once was the Commanding Officer of the Air Force Academy at Colorado Springs; and St. Clair Street who made a spectacular flight to Alaska, and many others.

At this time, having completed the course required of reserve officers, Paul was free to accept a job as test pilot while waiting his call to active duty. A new type of airplane, whose new feature was the changeable angle of incidence, was supposed to revolutionize the aircraft industry. It had been built by Whitman Brothers of Newark, N.J. for its inventor, Mr. Lanzius, and it was now ready for a test flight at a field on Long Island near Garden City. This was the scene of several historic flights by Glenn Curtiss and others and it later became Roosevelt Field. Paul went to Mineola and stayed at the Gold Bug Hotel, the haunt of pioneer flyers, and made preparations to fly the Lanzius in a cross-country race from New York to Chicago for which a $25,000 prize was at stake. Paul was skeptical about the plane's performance but since it was powered by a Deusenburg engine, he had complete confidence. After some weeks of alterations and test hops, they were ready for a trial flight. Paul succeeded in getting the big unwieldy thing a short way into the air, but the new feature didn't work and he landed upside down. The plane was rebuilt to correct its flaws and while preparing for a second try, army orders miraculously intervened. The Reserve Officers were called to duty, and Paul was ordered to report for overseas duty at once. As for the Lanzius, we were sorry to hear that later on a test pilot who also got it off the ground, but a bit farther than Paul, had crashed and was killed. That was the last we heard of the Lanzius machine.

12
The Early Birds

Years later, after his retirement, Paul had leisure time to pick up the threads of old ties with aviation pioneers and to begin to collect the mementos and pictures of the early days preparatory to presenting them to the National Air and Space Museum of the Smithsonian where each Early Bird has a portfolio.

Much of the historic data on pioneer aviation would have been lost had it not been for the Early Bird Society which had its origin at the Air Races in Chicago in 1928. A group of pioneer flyers headed by Jack Vilas and Ernest Jones got together and decided it was time to form an organization to keep track of pioneer flyers, to work out some safe place to store and exhibit their records, historic data, souvenirs, and pictures and to preserve these for posterity before it should be too late. They also resolved to bring all possible pressure to bear for the return of the original Wright airplane to the United States from England, where Orville Wright had allowed it to be shipped after a misunderstanding with the Smithsonian Institute about the wording on a plaque placed there in memory of Dr. Langley, another pioneer of aviation.

Through the tireless efforts of the Early Birds and other interested groups, this was finally accomplished. On December 17, 1948, the Early Birds attended the celebration, as guests of honor, when the original Wright airplane was unveiled in the Smithsonian Institution, where it now hangs with this inscription:

THE ORIGINAL WRIGHT BROTHERS AEROPLANE
The world's first power-driven heavier-than-air machine
in which man made free, controlled and sustained flight.
Invented and built by Wilbur and Orville Wright.
Flown by them at Kitty Hawk, North Carolina,
December 17, 1903.

This precious historic relic which initiated a new era in world history has been miraculously protected for posterity. But it had barely missed being lost. It had been stored in the Wright's bicycle shop, had gone through the Dayton flood, and had been constantly exposed to the threat of fire and other dangers since it was shipped from Kitty Hawk back to Dayton in 1903. It had been loaned to the Massachusetts Institute of Technology in Boston in 1916 by permission of Orville Wright, and later it hung in the entrance of the first Pan American Air Show at Grand Central Palace in New York City in February, 1917.

It has always seemed regrettable to me that the Wright brothers' home and bicycle shop were allowed to be moved from their original location in Dayton to Greenfield Village at Dearborn, Michigan. Nevertheless, this was done and in April, 1938, 35 years after Kitty Hawk, Henry Ford invited the Early Birds along with many famous persons in aviation circles to the dedication. At this time the Early Birds were offered ample space in Edison Institute in Greenfield Village to exhibit their historic relics. Not only would this material have good and reverent care there, but it would be appropriately near the Wright home and bicycle shop. Today a great deal of Early Bird material can be seen there was well as at the Air Museum at Dayton, Ohio, and the Smithsonian.

The guest of honor at the dedication was Orville Wright. Charles E. Taylor, the mechanic who had worked with the Wrights in all their early experiments was also present. It was a reunion for two of the most famous Early Birds, Orville Wright and his pupil Brigadier General Frank P. Lahm who also was part of America's aviation history from the beginning. He held Army pilots license No. 1, and was affectionately known as Mr. Early Bird or Early Bird No. 1 by the entire aviation world. No one had done more to hold the group together and advance its interest than did he and Early Birds honored him at every gathering.

The special attention always given that venerable gentleman was his due, although no one was more modest about his accomplishments than Frank Lahm. He lived a long and useful life and his name is now included in the "In Memorium" of the Early Bird roster along with many others.

It is hard to imagine the progress aviation had made since 1903 for it changes so rapidly nowadays that the pioneers are often lost sight of in the momentum of the ever increasing and unfolding miracle of flight. But so it has ever been with pioneers. Most people cannot remember a time when there was no such thing as an airplane. They cannot imagine rushing into the street and gazing in wonder at the sight of the one lone airplane in the sky; nor believe that the pioneer aviator was regarded as almost superman — or as having all the glamor of a movie star. The only reaction one is apt to get from the present generation, when an airplane flies overhead, is perhaps a comment about the momentary disturbance it causes on his television screen!

With the passage of years, the wisdom and foresight of the Early Bird organization becomes more apparent. This has been proven beyond the fondest hopes of the handful of pioneer airmen who drew up the Early Bird charter, elected its first officers, and designed the certificate to be issued to all members who could qualify by proving that they had soloed before December 17, 1916, that historic December date that runs all through aviation manuals.

The charter reads, "Membership shall be limited to those who piloted a glider or airplane, gas balloon or airship prior to December 17, 1916, upon evidence deemed sufficient by the membership committee and approved by the Board of Governors; except that nationals and countries other than the United States engaged in World War I, must have met the foregoing conditions prior to August 4, 1914."

Very soon after the Early Bird organization was founded, 64 airmen had qualified, and by 1939 there were more than 350 members on the roster. Many began to attend the annual meetings which were held at the Air Races and to take an interest in its proceedings and to get acquainted with each other or to keep in touch through their little trade magazine appropriately called "Chirp." After the Air Races were discontinued, the Early Birds chose their own time and place for their reunions and they are still held each year. Beside their business meeting, there is a banquet to which the wives and families are invited. The festivities begin with a silent toast to their departed members; followed by speeches given by prominent airmen, business men, and government officials. Then comes the roll call which is the highlight of the evening, for each Early Bird rises in answer to his name, so his feathered friends can get a good look at him; then he gives a brief biographical sketch of his aviation career. That brings out many a harrowing tale of pioneer days, as well as many a laugh. Paul always began his story with a tribute to Captain Baldwin, and also enjoyed telling about his experiences in the First Air Mail, of the many humorous as well as hazardous episodes in this service. These were the people who in their youth when full of hopes and dreams, helped to blaze the trail for the development of the aircraft industry in the pioneer period between 1903 and 1916. Fittingly, and lest we forget, a timely honor was paid to them when a bronze plaque with their 593 names inscribed (the final tabulation) was unveiled and dedicated on April 16, 1962 in the Air and Space Building of the National Air Museum of the Smithsonian, at a ceremony which many Early Birds attended. The inscription on the tablet reads: *"TO THE EARLY BIRDS, COMMEMORATING WITH RESPECT AND REVERENCE THE SIGNIFICANT CONTRIBUTION TO THE HISTORY OF FLIGHT MADE BY THESE PILOTS WHO FLEW SOLO BEFORE DECEMBER 17, 1916."*

I did not know all the Early Birds but I feel a kinship to them because of all I learned at these banquet recitals, but I have some first hand knowledge of many of the biographies such as Walter E. Lees. He and his wife Loa, our treasured friends for many years, were often companions at the Air Races and at the reunions. Walter was one of the real old timers, who started his aviation career with Tom Benoist in St. Louis in 1911, then went to North Island, San Diego, California, to learn to fly a Curtiss Flying boat.

Walter had been lured away from the University of Wisconsin in his sophomore year by this "Lorelei" aviation. He and Jimmy Johnson, another close friend, met at North Island and struggled through their early flying days together. Although Jimmy had graduated from college — even to earning his master's degree in mechanical engineering at Purdue — yet neither one had worked long enough to lay aside funds adequate to pay for flying lessons. More than once they flipped a coin to see whether it would be a few minutes flying instruction or a good square meal. It was most often the former, and they subsisted on a diet of bananas and milk. Among Walter's more publicized aviation achievements was the establishment of the world's first non-refueling endurance record at Jacksonville Beach, Florida in May, 1931. His co-pilot was Frederick A. Brossy. This test proved the worth of the Packard airplane engine, a new invention of Captain Woolson's. The Packard company was unable to continue work on that engine after Captain Woolson's untimely and tragic death in an airplane crash. As for Walter Lees: as a Reserve Navy Commander he saw active duty in World War II and later retired to his ranch in California where he lived until his death.

One of the most active of the Early Birds was Augustus Post. Aviation lost one of its most colorful characters in his passing. Beside being the thirteenth man in the United States to fly an aeroplane, he was a pioneer balloon racer; one of the first auto racers; and an actor who frequently took parts in Broadway plays. He was a writer, publisher, poet and co-founder of the Aero Club of America. He was a witty reconteur, among his favorite tales being the one about the balloon race in which he competed in about the year 1900, when his balloon burst over Berlin and he descended 3,000 feet in his parachute, landing on a rooftop right outside a ladies boudoir window! You could spot Augustus Post in any crowd. He wore a mustache and goatee which gave him a striking resemblance to Buffalo Bill. He used to say his goatee was a sign of patriotism because Uncle Sam wears one. He kept a voluminous scrap book which he brought to all reunions and he was a walking encyclopedia on the subject of aviation.

He was proud to have pioneered the automobile, too. In one of his letters to us dated February 28, 1948, he said "We are looking forward to next year's air races. I am sure we'll have the same good time. Sorry to lose Orville and Dick Depew," and he enclosed a pen sketch of himself driving a Winton car in a race from New York to Chicago in 1904. He is pictured wearing the conventional linen duster, goggles, and gauntlets of the period.

Another famous name in Early Bird annals is that of Commander E.W. Spencer, one of the pioneer aviators of the United States Navy, whose first wife was Wallis Warfield, later the Duchess of Windsor.

Then there is Early Bird Burt "Fish" Hassell, another old-timer who was better known as retired Colonel B.R.J. Hassell, especially to those young flyers of the Ferry Command, in World War II, whose welfare he was responsible for at Gander, Newfoundland. He was a natural for that assignment, having done pioneer flying in the Arctic area before most of these modern pilots were born. Years ago, in 1928, his home town of Rockford, Illinois sponsored a flight to Sweden to be made by "Fish" and a friend named Parker Cramer. Newspapers all over the world carried the story of the project and its successful take-off. But the plane, named "The Greater Rockford," disappeared somewhere over Greenland, and for days the flyers were given up for lost. An anxious family and his friends waited for word of the plane, when suddenly a message came that the flyers were alive and safe. The plane, out of gas, had made an emergency landing and had to be abandoned. Cramer was severly injured and Fish carried him out to civilization after days of struggle through the icy wasteland, thereby saving both their lives. This trek earned for Fish the title "The Hiking Viking."

Little did Fish dream he would ever see his little Stinson again but after 40 years he was to realize the "impossible dream." The melting snow and ice had repeatedly uncovered and revealed the wreckage of the airplane to the many pilots who flew over that northern route on routine schedule. However it did not seem necessary, practical nor safe to try to dislodge it from the icy grip of an arctic peak and rescue it. But the time came for a group of Fish's friends, accompanied by two of his sons, to do just that, to rescue it by means of a helicopter. That brave crew flew to the area in a Sikorsky S-61 N helicopter, unbolted the wings, strapped them to the fuselage, secured it all with heavy cables and hoisted the bundle aboard the helicopter and flew it to Sondre, Stromfjord, Greenland in September, 1968. From there it was flown by cargo plane back to Rockford to eventually be rebuilt.

Although Fish had made a perfect landing on that ice cap, the plane was on its back when rescued. The hurricane winds of the north had tipped it over, damaging the wings in the process but the rescuers were amazed to find the fuselage practically intact, its name "The Greater Rockford" plainly visible and with all gear, equipment and the log still intact, preserved by the deep freeze. The Hassell sons told me they were surprised to find the doors of the cockpit locked — a queer precaution to take in that desolate waste land. Heaven only knows who would disturb their possessions on that forbidden peak 4000 feet above sea level.

News of the recovery of "The Greater Rockford" was flashed around the world and messages poured in from friends from near and far. Its return was like the return of the native, and no one was more thrilled to see it come home than Fish. Friends rallied to rebuilding the historic relic, much as they did when the Air Mail plane "Old No. 259" was recovered from a similar mountain-top crash. To help restore it became a community labor-of-love in Santa Paula, California where it was rebuilt in the spring of 1968 in preparation for the Golden Anniversary of the inauguration of the air mail service.

As I have listened to the Early Bird tales from year to year and watched new planes become progressively more efficient, I am amazed at the phenomenal growth of the aircraft industry in the few short years since the world thought it couldn't be done. First in the evolution of the airplane was the powered bipline with the pilot lying prone on the lower wing controlling it by a pair of levers. Later came a standardized system of controls on all planes called the "Dep" control for the Frenchman, Depedussin, who invented it. It was a mechanism which coordinated ailerons and elevator controls with the rudder-bar which was operated by the feet. Then came dual control with a tandem seat for pilot and passenger or student. Then as military, air mail and commercial aviation evolved, and more and more passengers were carried, there was need for pilot, co-pilot and crew to man the big planes. What Early Bird would have dared predict in 1916 that one day in the future he would fly non-stop in a commercial airplane from coast to coast and even beyond in a comfortable pressurized cabin and with delicious hot meals served.

Imagine, at the turn of the century, a distinguished scientist said, "To carry a single man from place to place in the air, at pleasure, would require the discovery of some new metal or some new force."

Even Thomas Edison wrote in an article in the Scientific American, November, 1902, "There are no known facts by which one could predict any commercial future for aerial navigation."

Another "doubting Thomas" was a Rear Admiral who submitted this report on flying: "A calm survey of certain natural phenomena leads the engineer to pronounce all confident prophesies at this time, for the future success of flying as wholly unwarranted, if not absurd." Someone else said, not without sarcasm, "The North Pole and the interior of the Sahara Desert can preserve their secrets a while longer."

As far back as the seventeenth century a protest against military aviation was voiced by Deodata Francesco Lana (1631-87) in an essay called "The Bomber." He must have taken a prophetic look into the twentieth century and seen the bombings of the world wars and of the present conflicts. He wrote: "God would prohibit such a war. On the day of a decisive battle, what use would there be to have a mutilated civilian population of the enemy who take no effective part in the fighting, leaving helpless women, children, and old people to cause panic," a theory which, alas, was soon to be discounted. They gave us much to think about as the days sped on through winter to the spring of 1917 when the United States entered the European War to make the world safe for democracy.

At the celebration of the golden anniversary of flight in Washington in 1953, the Early Birds were visited in their box by such famous flyers as Eddie Rickenbacker, the late Roscoe Turner, and Jacqueline Cochran. Their familiar names along with Jimmy Doolittle, Richard Byrd, Charles Lindbergh, and others, are the ones best known perhaps to the public today as our pioneer aviators. But many of the Early Birds antedated all of them, and as such, were honored guests seated near the speaker's platform where the flyers who were participating in the event, made it a point to call on them.

It is always easy to spot an Early Bird at any gathering of birdmen because of the black and white checkered caps they wear. The checkered cap became the insignia of the Early Birds because in the early days Lincoln Beachey wore a cap like that with the visor turned around, whenever he flew exhibitions, and it caught the fancy of aviators, and of the public. The checkered cap gave the Early Birds preferential treatment at the Air Races especially after the loud speaker would call attention to them and to the box in which they were seated. Many of the spectators had never heard of any of the Early Birds, although they had made headlines regularly in their day, until the announcer told the crowd "the men in the checkered caps were the surviving airmen who pioneered aviation, thus making today's races possible," and that they were the men who lived to tell the tale from Jennies to Jets to Rockets to Spacecraft.

It was exciting being an Early bird wife in the pioneer days, and now as an Associate member of the Early Birds of Aviation and of the Air Mail Pioneers, I feel I am a part of those organizations, because my husband and I went through all of the pioneer experiences together, sharing the ups and downs (some literally) with such rapport that I feel I can claim a spot in the "nest." I felt this bond with the Early Birds keenly at their annual meeting in Los Angeles in October 1966 when I had the great honor of receiving a bronze plaque awarded posthumously to my husband H. Paul Culver, commemorating the 50th year since his solo flight. Each Early Bird receives this on the golden anniversary of his solo, and he treasures it with pride and affection. I truly regretted that Paul was not there to receive his from the hand of his flying instructor Carl Batts who was the current President of the Early Birds.

13
The Golden Anniversary

No one would have enjoyed the Golden Anniversary of the First Air Mail held in Washington on May 15, 1968, more than Paul. It would have given him the opportunity to talk over old times with Reuben Fleet. And it would have been his pleasure to again see Jim Edgerton and his wife Mary, whom we had not seen since the Fortieth Anniversary when Jim unveiled the marker in Potomac Park, commemorating his landing there on that historic day in 1918. And now Jim was the only one of the original Army pilots who flew the mail on that day present at the Golden Anniversary.

The U.S. Air Mail Pioneers had been preparing for this event for several years under the leadership of its president Luke Harris, with the cooperation of such air mail pioneers as J.W. (Bill) Hackbarth of Santa Paula, California, who had a dream and a plan. Being familiar with the historic air mail routes as they spread out over the west from 1918 to 1927, Bill remembered hearing pilots tell of sighting the wreckage of one of those old planes on a mountain top known as Porcupine Ridge, near Coalville, Utah. Bill knew it was air mail plane Old No. 249 which had crashed in a Rocky Mountain storm on December 15, 1922, and that its pilot had been Henry G. Boonstra who was still living in Salt Lake City. Henry had salvaged his bag, his compass and maps, and made his perilous way down the mountain in the bitter cold. It was 36 hours before he reached a ranch house where Ross Rigby took him in, attended to his needs, and insisted that he rest there for a few days before proceeding on his journey down the mountain to home-base at Salt Lake City. Days later after being given up as lost, his return was proclaimed a miracle.

During the next few days, several airplanes searched for the downed mail plane. On the third day it was spotted, and a route mapped out for a searching party to climb the mountain and recover the mail. When they reached it, they saw that Old No. 249 had made a permanent landing and so it had to be abandoned. There it lay for years, through all kinds of weather, while its frail parts disintegrated and only the metal parts survived. Even these parts had been picked over by hunters and trappers. But there was enough left to inspire Bill Hackbarth to make a trip to Salt Lake city in the fall of 1964, to discuss with Henry Boonstra a plan that he had to salvage the wreckage, transport it to his ranch at Santa Paula, rebuild it and fly it to Washington to present to the Smithsonian in honor of the Golden Anniversary. Hank Boonstra cooperated and gave Bill all the details about the location of the wreckage. Bill flew over the area, spotted the wreckage and began to make plans to climb up to it by truck the next spring. It was already too late in the fall to make the trip.

With the coming of spring Bill made his way up the narrow trail to a clearing where a sheep herder lived who knew of the pile of wreckage. He cautioned Bill against attempting to reach it with his truck, so he offered to gather up all the pieces and bring them down the next time he got near the spot with his Jeep, and he would let Bill know when this was accomplished. And so that is how Old No. 249 got into Bill Hackbarth's hands — all 600 pounds of pieces, which became the nucleus of the beautiful air mail plane which once had a place at the Smithsonian.

But it was not all smooth sailing for Old No. 249 even after it rested under the protection of Bill Hackbarth's shop at Santa Paula. After it was partially assembled, and missing parts had been donated by aviation antique-collectors and many volunteer man-hours had gone into its resur- . rection, suddenly in the fall of 1967 a brush fire swept the area, crept up to the Hackbarth ranch, and devoured Bill's shop with Old No. 249 in it. Again it was reduced to a skeleton. Such a tragedy would have overwhelmed and discouraged most anyone else, but Bill and the other Air Mail Pioneers accepted the challenge and went back to the job of rebuilding. A notice about the tragedy was sent out at once to all of the Air Mail Pioneers and they rallied around Bill Hackbarth with donations of money, man-hours and spare parts, some of which had been hoarded for years in barns and garages. And so it was that with the encouragment and cooperation of his friends and his wife, Gladys, Bill again set to work to rebuild Old No. 249.

By mid April 1968, it was ready to test fly and plans were made to fly it across the country, by easy stages, following the route of the old maps, making the same relay stops over an 18 day period and arrive in Washington in time for the Golden Anniversary. Some refinements were added to a 40 year old airplane in order for it to take to the well traveled skyways of the modern age, and to conform to F.A.A. standards. Up-to-date instruments, radio, and brakes were added, and a flight pattern worked out to coordinate with the ground crew which was to accompany Bill across the country in automobiles. Ed Jewel drove a truck with spare parts, and John Lunsford, accompanied by his 12 year old grandson Jeff Cox, went along in another car to supervise any needed repair. This was a three car caravan, for Gladys Hackbarth drove her car solo all the way and waited for her husband at each of the relay points. She was an important part of this sentimental journey of 3000 miles.

And so it was that Bill Hackbarth's dream came true: to fly Old No. 249 over the original cross-country air mail routes to Washington. It was accomplished without a hitch, except for one slight error when he touched down at the Anacosta Naval Air Station instead of at the Washington National Airport. He quickly realized his mistake and took off at once, flying to where the crowd waited. He landed alongside a huge jet, which dwarfed Old No. 249, and by contrast illustrated the great strides aviation had made in the intervening years.

The press picked up this wrong landing episode and stressed that more than the fact that Bill had made the flight all the way without a mishap. Perhaps that kind of story appeals more to the reading public which seems to demand the sensational rather than the conventional. Many of the stories that were printed commemorating the first Air Mail gave more space to the failure of Lieutenant Boyle's part in the start of the service, than to the successful flights made by Edgerton, Webb, and Culver.

The task of knocking down Old No. 249 to transport it to the Smithsonian was the next step. This was done by aviation mechanics under the direction of its builder and pilot with the assistance of its original air mail pilot, Hank Boonstra. These men were assisted by Paul Garber, who because of his position at the Smithsonian, was familiar with such projects and had arranged every phase of the transfer. He had supervised the placing of many valuable historic and priceless exhibits there, but this time it was a special and also personal project. Consequently, the transfer and assembling was all done with dispatch, so that on the day before the formal presentation, it was ready for the preview by the U.S. Air Mail Pioneers. Among the most interested were Reuben Fleet and Jim Edgerton who commented that it was not the type they flew on the inauguration flights fifty years ago. They flew Curtiss Jennies. This De Haviland which supplanted the Jenny when the civilians took over looked much sturdier with its plywood fuselage instead of a cloth covered one, and with its powerful Liberty motor instead of the Hispano Suiza engine of far less horsepower.

The most famous of the early air mail pilots who dropped in for the preview was Charles Lindbergh. He came early in the morning and was very impressed with Old No. 249, inspecting it with Paul Garber acting as host and guide. What a pity he did not feel free to stay and mingle with the other air mail pioneers and to appear at the formal ceremonies the next day. Had he wished to take part he might have quoted from his classic story "The Spirit of St. Louis": "We pilots of the mail have a tradition to establish. The commerce of the air depends on it. Men have already died for that tradition. Every division of the mail routes had its hallowed points of crash where some pilot on a stormy night, or lost and blinded by fog, laid down his life on the altar of his occupation."

The committee which had formulated all the plans for the Golden Anniversary was headed by its President, Luke Harris on the west coast, and Major General Brooke T. Allen in Washington. They gave the name "GAMA" to the project. This abbreviation did not, however, suggest a curtailed program, which began with the unveiling of the sketch of the commemorative stamp which would go on sale May 15, and was previewed by the U.S. Air Mail Pioneers in February 1968. Plans for the Air Mail week followed and included sight-seeing tours, banquets, cocktail parties, informal get-togethers, but "mutual admiration" sessions did not have to be scheduled, because whenever old pilots get together they love to tell of their early exploits and need no encouragement. The plans included having the Willard Hotel as headquarters. Nothing could have suited them better than to have their reunion in this famous and centrally located landmark which had been the home of Presidents, Senators and dignitaries, both foreign and domestic and which had been the center of the social whirl in the capital for a century. The first President to stay there was Franklin Pierce who moved in in November 1852, and stayed until his inauguration the following March 4. James Buchanan, Abraham Lincoln, William Howard Taft, Woodrow Wilson, Calvin Coolidge, and Warren Harding had all made their homes there for periods of time.

But there was a more personal reason for my attachment to this lovely old hotel: it had been the scene of my marriage to a pioneer airman 50 years before. But now, so-called progress decreed that the Willard was to be closed so it seemed fitting that one of the final conventions it hosted was the Golden Anniversary of the Air Mail. As buildings outlive their usefulness so do eras, for as Major General Brooke Allen remarked: "The importance of this celebration lies in the fact that if first class mail service merges with the present air mail service, there will be no more air mail anniversaries to celebrate."

If this was to be the final anniversary, it was indeed the best, and the grand finale was the ceremony at the Smithsonian on May 15, 1968 when Old No. 249 was formally presented as the U.S. Air Mail Pioneer's gift to posterity. These pioneers along with their families entered the great Hall that historic morning through the entrance above which hung the original Wright airplane. It was flanked on one side by Lindbergh's "The Spirit of St. Louis" and on the other side by Wiley Post's "Winnie Mae." Ahead we could see Old No. 249 with a dozen spotlights on it. The Marine band struck up a stirring march and the assembled audience stood at attention as the Pioneer Air Mail pilots marched in and took their places in front of the row of speakers who were to extol the merits of those hardy pioneers of aviation. Postmaster General W. Marvin Watson greeted them and then read a message from President Johnson. Mr. Watson then gave a short history of the air mail, giving credit to Major Reuben Fleet. Major Fleet in his turn gave full credit to his air mail pilots and crew. Dr. George Connor who had been Assistant Postmaster Otto Praeger's chief clerk at the time the air mail was started, was then introduced. It was he who had arranged a pilgrimage of pioneer air mail men to the grave of Otto Praeger in Fort Lincoln cemetery on the outskirts of Washington and told us of his dream to make the delivery of mail up-to-date by using airplanes to transport it and Ford trucks for its pick-up instead of horse and wagon then in use. His persistent effort to expand air mail routes and not let the service die when both the government and public lost interest in it, is credited with having laid the foundation of commercial aviation as it exists today. To have abandoned air mail during the slump that followed World War I would have set aviation back for years.

Jim Edgerton was next to take a bow for he was the only one of the original four present. Then, much to my surprise, the speaker said: "And last but not least, we have with us the wife of Lieutenant H. Paul Culver who was the pilot who flew the world's first regularly scheduled air mail to New York City on May 15, 1918, and she was there to witness that historic event. Will she please stand up." I did so, proudly, in silent salute to Paul. I am proud to have been the wife of a U.S. Air Mail Pioneer. Later the Post Office Department was kind enough to present me with a handsome leather portfolio with my name engraved in gold and containing a hundred first-day stamps commemorating the Golden Anniversary.

When the presentation ceremony was over and the Smithsonian had formally accepted Bill Hackbarth's gift, we all bade farewell to Old No. 249. We understood how Bill Hackbarth and Hank Boonstra felt when they said if they were not sure the Smithsonian would give it tender, loving care, they had a mind to fly it right back to California. However, they realized many more people would be able to see and admire the plane in this berth than if it were back in Santa Paula.

I feel sure that the Hackbarths, and perhaps some of the others, must have gone back to the Smithsonian on the day following the ceremonies for one last look at Old No. 249.

Later, when the National Air and Space Museum was added to the Smithsonian on July 4, 1976 to house the world's most extensive aircraft and spacecraft collection, and the original airplanes were moved to the new Great Hall, the mail plane, Old No. 249 was not among them. The reason given was that it was a rebuilt airplane and not an original and so did not meet the requirements. Some time later when the San Diego Aviation Museum was rebuilt after its tragic fire, Old No. 249 found an honored and permanent home there, where it can be seen by all who are interested in the saga of air mail, especially by the pilots who flew the mail, such as George Taylor, Glenn Messer, Jerome Lederer, Emil Henrich, Louis Krentz, Edwin Cooper and a host of others. Perhaps it is even more fitting to have the mail plane on exhibit in San Diego where the name of Reuben H. Fleet, the founder of air mail is so well known as an honored citizen, and where the Reuben H. Fleet Space Theater and Science Center stands as a lasting tribute to a remarkable name.

I could share that feeling for I too had a dream and a plan. It was to salvage something for posterity, even though less tangible. It was to write about the early days of aviation, to reclaim my aviation memories from the "mountain top" where they had been buried under the accumulation of life's experiences, of "storm and shine" for half a century, and to assemble and rebuild them into a book. In doing so I have had a nostalgic, though precious journey back into the past where I had the privilege of sharing some of the most thrilling and exciting years when aviation was in its infancy and to watch it grow and expand ever since.

Although I could not expect my reclaimed, historic memoirs to have a niche, such as Old No. 249 has, I knew that by placing them between the covers of a book I could share them with the public and preserve them. In doing so, I salute and honor all of the brave men and women who pioneered the air and space age.

Index

Aero Club of America, 16, 60-61
87, 114
Air Mail Pilots Convention, Reno,
1966, 43
Air Mail Pioneers, 67, 118-120, 122
Air Mail Service, 42-69
Golden anniversary of: 119-124
Air Mail Stamp, first, 56-57
Allen, Brooke T., 122-123
Allyn, Dave, 103
Arnold, H.H. ("Hap"), 44, 66
Atlantic Coast Experimental Station,
9, 16, 71, 85-86, 91, 99

Baker, Newton D., 44-45, 55
Baldwin Field, Quincy, Il., 98
Baldwin, Ivy, 94, 96
Baldwin Park, Quincy, Il., 96, 98
Baldwin, Thomas Scott, 16, 20, 71,
85, 87-91, 93-99, 108
Barnaby, Walter, 24-27, 108
Barnes, James, 28
Batts, Carl, 106
Beachey, Lincoln, 89, 117
Belmont, August, 45, 48, 66
Belmont Park, Long Island, NY, 45,
48, 61-62
Benoist, Tom, 113
Bishop, William, 36
Bonsal, Steve, 43, 47-48, 60, 63, 65
Boonstra, Henry G., 119-121, 124
Bouldin, William, 25-27
Boyle, George, 43, 47-48, 53-54,
57-58, 60-61, 63-64, 121
Brossy, Frederick A., 114
Bullock, Walter, 86
Bumbaugh, George L., 93
Burleson, A.S., 44, 55
Bustleton Field, PA., 48-53, 58, 64

Canady E.L., 42
Carlstrom, Carl, 107
Carlstrom, Victor, 86-87, 99, 107
Carter, James E., 108
Castle, Irene, 88
Castle, Vernon, 88
Christie, Arthur, 35-36
Cochran, Jacqueline, 117
Cogswell, Stewart, 99
Colgen, Bill, 108
Collier, Robert, 33
Colliers Magazine, 32-33
Conner, George L., 55, 124
Cooper, Edwin, 125
Cox, Jeff, 121
Cramer, Parker, 115
Culver, Edith, 39
Culver, H. Paul, 7, 16-17, 20-34,
36-38, 40-43, 46-54, 58-66, 68-76,
87-88, 90-92, 99-101, 105,
108-110, 113, 118, 121, 124
Culver, John, 39
Culver, Miller, 38
Culver, Paul Dodd ("Jim"), 33-34,
39, 41
Curry, John, 40
Curtiss Aeroplane and Motor Corp.,
45, 48
Curtiss Flying School, 9, 16, 19-20,
24, 29, 37, 71, 75, 85-88, 90, 92,
99, 107-108
Curtiss Glenn, 16, 46, 86, 88-89, 99,
104, 109

Daniels, Josephus, 55
Dawn, Hazel, 32
Day, Bill, 99
De La Vergne, Charles De Bony, 17
Deeds, E.A., 45

Depew, Dick, 114
Dodd, Helen, 71
Duesenburg, Fred, 105
Dunham, R.A., 88

Early Birds, of Aviation, 5-8, 16, 40,
    72-74, 94, 98, 110-118
Edgerton, Jim, 43, 47-50, 53-54,
    59-61, 63, 65, 68, 119, 121-122,
    124
Edison, Thomas, 116
Ellington Field, Houston, TX, 16-18,
    20, 24, 38-41, 52
Ely, Eugene, B., 91
Epps, Carey, 107

Firestone, Harvey, Jr., 34, 37
First Aero Squadron, 24-27
Fleet, David, 55
Fleet, Reuben, 43-57, 61, 64, 66, 68,
    119, 122-123, 125
Ford, Henry, 102, 111
Foulois, Benjamin, 30
Fowler, Robert G., 88

Gallop, Harold ("Buck"), 24-27
Garber, Irene ("Buttons"), 7
Garber, Paul E., 6, 55, 73, 121-122
Greenfield Village, 6, 111

Hackbarth, Gladys, 120-121
Hackbarth, J.W. (Bill), 119-121, 124
Haig, Emma, 32
Hall, Ernest, 37
Hamilton Watch Co. 61-62
Hare, James ("Jimmy") T., 32-33
Harris, Luke, 119, 122
Hartung, Harvey L., 63
Hassel, Burt ("Fish"), 99, 114-116
Havens, Beckwith, 11, 74, 89
Hawley, Allen, 60-61
Heermance, Andrew, 99
Henrich, Emil, 125
Honor, Jim, 99

Ivy, William SEE
    Baldwin, Ivy

Jackson, C.S., 36
Jewel, Ed, 121
Johnson, Jimmy, 25, 99, 113
Jones, Ernest, 110

Kenly, William L., 24
Kennson, E.R., 28
Kilgore, E.W., 64
Kirby, Maxwell, 36
Kirkham, Percy, 99
Kitty Hawk, NC, 5, 33, 35, 110
Krentz, Louis, 125

Lahm, Frank P., 111
Lana, Deodata Francesco, 117
Lane, Franklin K., 108
Lane, Franklin K., Jr., 108
Law, Ruth, 12
Lederer, Jerome, 125
Lees, Loa, 9, 92, 113
Lees, Walter E., 9, 25, 37, 75,
    99-100, 105, 113-114
Lindbergh, Charles, A., 7, 15, 67,
    117, 122-123
Lipsner, B.B., 56-58
Lone Wolf, The (movie), 32
Lunsford, John, 121
Lytell, Bert, 32

McCauley, J.B., 36
McChord, Charles C., 47
Mac Gordon, Steve, 87, 99
Messer, Glenn, 125
Miller, Charles, F., 61
Miller, Walter, 43, 47-48, 63, 65
Milling, Tom, 24, 88
Mills, Marshall, 28, 31
Mitchell, Johnny, 99
Mitchell, William (Billy), 24-27, 88,
    99-100
Mulvihill, Bill, 41
Mulvihill, Evelyn, 41

National Air and Space Museum,
    6, 110, 113, 124
Nelson, Paul, 29

Newton, Byron, 60-61
Novello, Ivor, 92

Olds, Robin, 108
Olds, Robert (Bob), 108
Otero, Michael, 103
Otero, Mrs. Michael SEE
   Stinson, Katherine
Ovington, Earl, 42
OX-5 Aviation Pioneers, 14

Packard Aircraft Co. 100, 114
Pan American Aeronautical
   Exposition, 1st, New York, NY,
   104, 111
Patton, Thomas G., 60
Paul E. Garber Preservation,
   Restoration and Storage Facility,
   Suitland, MD, 6
Polo Field, Washington, D.C., 46, 54
Pool, Caroline, 96
Post, Augustus, 114
Post, Wiley, 7, 123
Praeger, Otto, 44, 55, 124
Princeton Flying School, 28, 31
Princeton University, 27-34
Pyne, Percy, 28

Reuben H. Fleet Space Theater and
   Science Center, San Diego, CA,
   125
Rickenbacker, Eddie, 92, 102, 105,
   117
Rigby, Ross, 119
Robey, William T., 57
Robinson, Paul, 34, 37
Rolfe, William, 24-27
Roosevelt, Pres. Franklin D., 55, 66

Sales, Charles, 51-53
San Diego Aviation Museum, 125
Schauffler, William, (Bill) G., 24-27
Schroeder, Rudolph (Shorty), 101-103
Scott, Blanche Stuart, 11, 89
Shepard, Alan B., Jr., 39

Smythe, Sidney T., 29
Southee, Earl, 21-22, 37
Spencer, E.W., 114
Springs, Elliot White, 34
Stanton, Frank, 28
Stinson, Eddie, 23
Stinson, Katherine, 12-13, 23,
   100-101, 103
Stinson, Marjory, 23

Taussig, Noah, 56
Taylor, Charles E., 90, 111
Taylor, George, 125
Turner, Roscoe, 117

U.S. Air Mail Pioneers SEE
   Air Mail Pioneers
U.S. Signal Corps, 16, 24-27, 29

Vaughn, Stanley, 99
Vernon, Charlotte, 9
Vernon, Victor, 9, 20, 36-37, 71
   87, 91, 99
Victoria, Queen, 96-97
Vilas, Jack, 110

Ward, Jimmy, 74
Watson, W. Marvin, 123
Webb, Torrey, 43, 46-48, 59-60,
   62-63, 68, 121
Wheaton, Ivan P., 37
Wilbur Wright Field, Dayton, OH,
   34-37, 40
Wilson, Mrs. Woodrow, 55, 58, 68
Wilson, Pres. Woodrow, 30, 42-44,
   55-58, 70, 105, 123
Woodhouse, Henry, 61
World War I, 16-17
Wright, Katharine, 10, 35
Wright, Milton, 35
Wright, Orville, 5-7, 30, 33, 35-36,
   61, 90, 110-111, 114
Wright, Wilbur, 5-7, 30, 33, 35-37,
   61, 90, 110
Wyson, Forrest, 73